"Tim writes like he preaches—from Scripture. Surely, if we're going to find release from worry, we must find the One who is greater than us. Tim points us to him in this well-written, easily-studied book."

BOB INGLIS, former Member of Congress

"This is the best book I have ever read on the frequently debilitating subject of worry. I started this book worrying about whether it would help me. But throughout the book, I found myself worshiping the Lord for who he is and what he does for his people... and, while worshiping, I found myself less anxious."

DR SAMUEL LOGAN, International Director, The World Reformed Fellowship

"In *Living Without Worry*, Tim Lane provides a unique combination of understanding and compassion for the many worries of life along with a God-focused, Christ-centered, eternal orientation. Tim offers every reader a robust diagnosis of worry and a heart-centered, biblical, and relevant prescription for replacing anxiety with peace."

DR BOB KELLEMEN, VP of Institutional Development, Crossroads Bible College; author of *Anxiety: Anatomy and Cure*

"I worry. All my attempts to stop worrying have failed pitifully in the past, leaving me even more vexed, but finally there's a book that can help break that cycle. Tim Lane gets to the heart of what worry is and why we all do it, and gently shows us a better, more biblical, way to live, saturated in the grace of the gospel. An accessible must-read for anyone who wants to begin the journey of worrying less."

HELEN THORNE, Training Manager at London City Mission; author of *Purity is Possible*

"Timothy Lane speaks biblically and personally to our struggles with worry. I recommend this readable yet profound book to all who grapple with life in the midst of an uncertain world."

TREMPER LONGMAN III, Professor of Biblical Studies, Westmont College, Santa Barbara, California

"Tim writes simply but not simplistically, with sympathy and yet without letting us off the hook. Whether you're beset with worries or are seeking to help others who are, this is a great read. It probably won't stop you worrying, but it will give you a framework for understanding it and some strategies for dealing with it."

RICHARD UNDERWOOD, Pastoral Ministries Director, The Fellowship of Independent Evangelical Churches

"Tim Lane's latest book is a classic! *Living Without Worry* is theologically robust, laced with wisdom, filled with the love and grace of God, and intensely practical. After reading it, I went through it again, making notes to share with friends and remember myself. We all struggle with worry; Tim has provided a strategy to help us grow spiritually through the experience."

BOB D. DUKES, President and Executive Director of the Worldwide Discipleship Association; author of *Maturity Matters: The Priority and Process for Disciple Building in the Church*

"With great pastoral concern and a sharp biblical understanding of the problem, Tim Lane shows us how the Scriptures speak to the worries of our hearts. I will be using this book myself and recommending it to many."

SALLY ORWIN LEE, Executive Committee, Biblical Counseling UK

"*Living Without Worry* tremendously helped me understand the roots, causes and effects of worry. It clearly addresses what the Bible says about overcoming worry and replacing it with peace and trust in God. I don't know of anyone not affected by worry; may God help you conquer those worries as you read this book."

CLYDE CHRISTENSEN, Quarterback Coach, Indianapolis Colts, 2002 – present

"Unlike some Christian books that can actually exacerbate the problem, this brief, grace-saturated book will help give struggling Christians guidance on how to address their tendency to worry. Relying mostly on Scripture, but open to the insights of contemporary science, this is well-informed, Christ-centered pastoral wisdom at its best."

DR ERIC L. JOHNSON, Professor of Pastoral Care, Southern Baptist Theological Seminary; Director of the Society for Christian Psychology

"Worry is one of the greatest thieves in history. It robs people of their joy, peace, relationships and health. We all know we shouldn't worry, but we still do. Timothy Lane addresses this head on with a helpful ,biblical, and practical approach. Whether you worry a little or a lot, this book has the remedy!"

DR RICHARD BLACKABY, president of Blackaby Ministries International; author of *Experiencing God Day by Day*

"Do you worry? Well, here is a book for you! Rather than give you superficial steps to stop anxiety, Tim reminds us of the big picture of God's message of hope in the middle of the 'what ifs' of life."

DR PHILIP G. MONROE, Professor of Counseling and Psychology, Biblical Theological Seminary, Pennsylvania

TIMOTHY LANE

LIVING WITHOUT WORRY

How to replace anxiety with peace

For Barbara

Livng Without Worry. *How to Replace Anxiety with Peace*
© Timothy Lane/The Good Book Company, 2015.

Published by
The Good Book Company
Tel (US): 866 244 2165
Tel (UK): 0333 123 0880
International: +44 (0) 208 942 0880
Email: info@thegoodbook.com / info@thegoodbook.co.uk

Websites:
North America: www.thegoodbook.com
UK: www.thegoodbook.co.uk
Australia: www.thegoodbook.com.au
New Zealand: www.thegoodbook.co.nz

ISBN: 9781909919372

Design by André Parker

Printed and bound by CPI Group (UK) Ltd, Croydon, CR0 4YY

Contents

1. Why Not Worry?

"I tell you, do not worry about your life, what you will eat
or drink; or about your body, what you will wear."

"So do not worry, saying, 'What shall we eat?' or 'What
shall we drink?' or 'What shall we wear?'"

"Do not worry about tomorrow, for tomorrow will worry
about itself. Each day has enough trouble of its own."

Matthew 6 v 25, 31, 34

So you picked up a book on worry and right away you find
yourself hearing Jesus tell you not to worry. Now you are really
worried! Do Jesus' words comfort you, or do they just make
you more troubled? Was your response: "This is fine if you are
Jesus, the Son of God, but not if you are me, a regular person
with a myriad of things to worry about"?

It is tempting to dismiss Jesus' command not to worry
as unrealistic in today's world, and unfair to expect of you.
Everyone has worries, and everyone does worry; so how can
Jesus expect you and me—in fact how can he *command*
you and me—not to worry? Surely he was only talking of a
simpler, agricultural age, not the complexities of 21st-century
life? Surely he didn't mean all worry?

And yet... this command from Jesus is clear and it is
universal: "I tell you, do not worry". What will we do with it?!

Strangled

Jesus' command may seem impossible to you right now; but wouldn't it be great if it weren't? The English word "worry" comes from an Old English word meaning "strangle." "Anxiety" comes from an Indo-German word referring to suffering from narrowing, tightening feelings in the chest or throat. They're actually very helpful words to describe the feelings of low-level worry and anxiety. I've not met anyone who doesn't know how that feels, and while it may become a familiar companion in our lives, it never becomes a welcome one.

So wouldn't it be great if there were a way to worry less, or in fact not to worry at all, in the midst of your struggles? What if Jesus really could enable you to fight anxiety in your life in substantial ways? Jesus' teaching in Matthew 6, and the whole Bible's teaching, was not meant to be a burden— to give you something else to worry about, so that you end up thinking: "Now I'm worried that I'm worrying!" No, as we'll see, he does want to be honest about the world you live in, and give you liberating reasons not to worry. He wants to meet you in the middle of the complications and concerns of life with his goodness, mercy, grace and power.

Jesus wants you to deal with your worry. He wants you not to worry anymore. And he wants to help you with that. It's worth asking: what is the alternative? It is important to see that not dealing with your worry has a significant impact on life. Here are a few effects of chronic worry on our bodies:

- Difficulty swallowing
- Dizziness
- Dry mouth
- Fast heartbeat
- Fatigue

- Headaches
- Inability to concentrate
- Irritability
- Muscle aches
- Muscle tension
- Nausea
- Nervous energy
- Rapid breathing
- Shortness of breath
- Sweating
- Trembling and twitching

Those are fairly low-level, and I imagine you recognize some of them from your own experience; but worry can also lead to more serious physical consequences:

- Suppression of the immune system
- Digestive disorders
- Muscle tension
- Short-term memory loss
- Premature coronary artery disease
- Heart attack

More importantly than all of this, though, is the truth that whenever you are struggling with any form of obedience, it is ultimately connected to your relationship with God. When you worry, you are not enjoying your relationship with God; you're missing a part of the joy and fullness that he promises to you.

In addition, worry will impact the way you relate to others. Worrying may appear to be an effective coping skill and it may even make you "feel" safe, but it will not produce fruit in your life. You will find yourself not taking opportunities that God is laying in front of you, because you are trapped by worrying about what might go wrong. You may find yourself holding back in your relationships with others, failing to love people and serve them, because you are worrying about getting hurt. And as we have already said, you may find that worrying is affecting your ability to sleep or impacting your health.

Worry Doesn't Work

The truth is that worry doesn't work. It seems natural to worry, maybe even loving to worry—but it doesn't change anything. "Can any one of you by worrying add a single hour to your life?" asks Jesus (v 27). Answer: *No!* Corrie Ten Boom, who sheltered Jews in German-occupied Holland in World War II and was then imprisoned in a concentration camp, knew more worrying circumstances than most; and she wrote: "Worry does not empty tomorrow of its sorrow. It empties today of its strength."

It may not seem possible to stop worrying; but it would be a positive thing to stop worrying, wouldn't it? That isn't easy; facing your worries will require from you the cost of real honesty and some hard work... but not facing your worries will cost you even more.

But to start with, let's remember that the reason Jesus is teaching us to not worry is because he knows that there are a lot of things that it seems very sensible to worry about! He actually acknowledges that "each day has enough trouble of its own" (v 34)! Jesus never says that life has no troubles, or that we should not care about them. He knows there is plenty of trouble that demands our attention and, yes, our worry. Is it possible that the Jesus who tells us not to worry also understands our plight more than we realize? I hope you will continue to read to find out.

The World is a Worrying Place

It was September 3, 2001, around 9 a.m. My wife, Barbara, and I, along with our four children, were visiting some friends in New York City. We had made our way up the elevator to the top floor of the Empire State Building and were comfortably and safely perched there, looking out over one of the most amazing cities in the world. We could see Central Park to our north. To our east was Long Island. To our west was New Jersey. And as we gazed south, there they were: the Twin Towers. It was an iconic view.

Later that day, we returned home to Philadelphia, and went back to our normal routines. Several days passed, until it was September 11, 2001. Comfort and safety were not a feature of that day. And that iconic view was no more. The United States, and the world, would never be the same.

As I have reflected on that infamous day, I am often stunned by how close my family was to this attack. Just eight days separated us from one of the worst attacks in our country's history! I often imagine what it would have been like if we had been on the Empire State Building at the time of the attack. What if the terrorists had chosen a date eight days earlier, and an equally iconic building in Manhattan: the one my family was standing at the top of?

When I consider that day, I become anxious. I worry. Why? Because the world you and I live in is unpredictable, dangerous and unsafe.

Prior to 9/11, I lived with the illusion that the world was a rather safe place. After that day, my thinking radically changed. It took 9/11 to shake me out of my false sense of safety and it caused me to become more anxious. For you, it may have been another day, and another event. Whatever it is, we all come to a point where we realize that the world we live in has many reasons to cause us worry.

See, once you start to think about it, there are all kinds of reasons to worry and struggle with anxiety. Over my many years of pastoring and counseling, I can say that there are countless people who struggle with worry because something difficult or even traumatic happened to them at some point in their lives. The memories are so clear that often things in the present can trigger those memories and cause them to spiral into a bout of anxiety. Life on this planet is unpredictable; cataclysmic tragedies, natural disasters, evil and accidents are happening all of the time. The surprising thing is not that there are a lot of anxious people in our world, but that there are not more! In one sense, to not worry seems to not be in touch with reality. The question isn't: "Why worry?" It is: "Why not worry?"

Daily Life is Full of Worry, Too

Let's bring this even closer to home. Large disasters and traumatic things can happen at any moment; but there are also the daily, mundane details of life that give us reason to struggle with anxiety. Let me share another personal story about my family.

Four months before 9/11, in the spring of 2001, I received a letter with a job offer that would require moving our family of six from South Carolina to Philadelphia—an 800-mile move. I took the job. It was a move we were really excited about; but it was a move that we were really anxious about, too.

- We worried about telling the church that I had been pastoring for ten years. How would they respond? Who would be my replacement?
- We worried about our children. They were ten, seven, three and two. Our ten-year-old daughter was at a

stage in her life where she was forming friendships at church and school. She was not enthusiastic about moving. Would she be OK? Were we doing the best thing for her?

- We worried about selling our home. Would it sell for a suitable price? Would it sell at all?! How long would it take? How much time and work would it take to prepare it for sale?
- We worried about buying a new home in Philadelphia. The cost of living was at least 30% higher than in South Carolina. The housing market was booming at the time and home prices were at their highest.
- We worried about finances and our budget. Could we afford it? How?

That was before we even moved! Once we reached Philadelphia, my worry only increased. I began to doubt whether I had made the right decision to uproot my family and leave a good job, nice house, friends and family. My anxiety turned into depression and I struggled with irritation, impatience and anger. I did not see it at the time, but my wife, Barbara, could tell that I was not doing well. It was not a good time.

We Are All Worriers

Why have I started by sharing some of my own personal story with you? Because I want you to know that I am in the trenches with you. I have chosen to share a few of the more common experiences to show you that you don't have to be a victim of a traumatic abuse to struggle with worry. We are all natural worriers; and studies suggest that around 40 million Americans are *chronic* worriers.

I know that the details of my life may not be similar to yours. I understand that the examples that I have shared may not be similar by degree to yours. You may even think that I have lived a rather charmed life based upon what I have shared. But the experience of worry knows no boundaries of wealth, education, career or gender. Remember, minor surgery still feels like major surgery if you are the patient. What might seem minor to you may be major to someone else.

In addition, I want you to see that just because I am writing a book on worry, it does not mean that I have overcome the struggle. I am facing various degrees of anxiety even as I write this book. Ironically, it involves another move, a new job, children who are struggling to adjust and finances that are in flux! This is life in a broken, fallen world. What I hope you will see throughout the pages of this book is a real person who needs help. I struggle with worry. I am in this with you, and I need daily encouragement and help, just like you. Just writing this book was a means by which God worked in my life to help me face up to, and then face down, some of the things I tend to worry about.

It may be that you are reading this book as someone who is not a Christian, but who senses that just maybe there is something in the Christian message and perspective that holds the key to getting help for your worries. In that case, I believe you're right to sense that! And I hope you come to see that you're right as you read what the Bible says about your life, and your worries.

It may be that you are reading this as someone who does call yourself a Christian, but you're unsure what that means (if anything) for the whole area of worry. Or you know that your faith should make a difference to your reaction to circumstances and that you shouldn't worry as much; yet just knowing that is not much use, as again and again you find that you are struggling with worry.

It may be that you not only struggle with worry like everyone, but that your struggle is as a result of something, or some things, that have happened to you in your past. It could be last month or many years ago. Depending on the severity of that event, your struggle with anxiety will be more intense. We will pick up on this cause of anxiety in chapter 4. But if this is you, then I want to say at the outset that the truths I point to and seek to apply in this book may not take your anxiety away completely; but they can begin to, and can enable you to continue with your life, loving God and serving others without walking under the burden of a constant or recurring crippling anxiety.

Whoever you are, since all of us know what it is to worry, this book is for *you*. Whether it is a relationship, a job, finances, sickness, loss, a season of grief, a traumatic event or anything else that has you worried as you read these words, my ultimate desire is for you to find, in relationship with Jesus, a new and renewed energy and resolve for the tasks and challenges that you are facing.

In the following chapters, you will be introduced to a perspective, truths and promises that have been and continue to be immensely helpful to me, and to many I have pastored and counseled over the years. As I wrote this book, real faces crossed my mind—faces of people who needed help and hope in the midst of deep worry. I was also reminded of how God worked in my life and in theirs to bring gradual but certain change into their lives. Sometimes, their circumstances changed; often, they did not. But one thing remained constant: God was present and worked in gracious and encouraging ways. It has been a privilege to walk with these people and to receive their encouragement as well. My hope is that you, too, will gain insight into how God is with you and how he can help you grow. Growth is a process, often gradual, and never achieved by "Six easy steps to [fill in your desire here]." By God's kindness and grace, change and growth are possible, even in something as ingrained and almost instinctive as worry and fear.

There are so many reasons to worry. Jesus knows that. After all, his life was not a walk in the park, but a walk toward execution. He lived in this world and faced the same struggles as us. He knows; he understands. And yet we return at the end of this chapter to where we started. In a world where there are so many things to worry about, Jesus was able to say:

"Do not worry."

Wouldn't it be wonderful if that were possible, and if Jesus were able to show us how it is? In the middle of a world of worry, that is what this book is about.

Questions for Reflection

1. What is happening in your life right now that causes you to struggle with worry? What do you tend to worry about in general?

2. Are there any events in your past that make you more prone to worry? If so, what are they?

3. When you worry, how does that impact the way you live, and how you relate to others?

4. What specific things (both positive and negative) do you do in order to deal with worry in your life?

5. Was there anything in this chapter that stood out for you, and raised questions that you had not had before?

2. What is Worry?

wor·ry

verb

1. give way to anxiety or unease; allow one's mind to dwell on difficulty or troubles.

Synonyms: fret, be concerned, be anxious, agonize, overthink, brood, panic, lose sleep, get worked up, get stressed, get in a state, stew, torment oneself

noun

2. a state of anxiety and uncertainty over actual or potential problems.

Synonyms: anxiety, perturbation, distress, concern, uneasiness, unease, disquiet, fretfulness, restlessness, nervousness, nerves, agitation, edginess, tension, stress, apprehension, fear, dread, trepidation, misgiving, angst.
Informal: butterflies (in the stomach), the willies, the heebie-jeebies

Diagnosis matters. Imagine you are feeling unwell, so you go to the doctor and he concludes, after asking you a number of questions, that you have a very bad cold. He prescribes rest, lots of liquids, and some cough medicine. Months later, you are still feeling terrible, and your cough is worse. You return again to your doctor, and he decides to run some tests. After they are sent back, it becomes apparent that actually you do not have a cold; you have lung cancer. The original diagnosis was a serious mistake.

When something is wrong, you need to know what you are dealing with. And that works for spiritual issues, too. For treatment to work, good diagnosis matters.

Defining Worry

So, what exactly is worry or anxiety (I will use the words "worry" and "anxiety" interchangeably in this book)? It's a condition common to virtually every human, in every society. Not many people are truly care-free. But what is worry?! Psychiatrist John Nemiah wrote in his article on "Anxiety States" in the *Comprehensive Textbook of Psychiatry*: "Mental and bodily functions find in anxiety a meeting place that is unparalleled in other aspects of human life". Allan V. Horwitz, in *Anxiety: A Short History*, says: "Factors related to biology, psychology, life history, and social and natural environments are omnipresent potential causes of anxiety."

While these various factors and components are very important, the Bible cuts even deeper, because it says that worry is a deeply spiritual issue. This is not to say that the Bible ignores or disputes the mental, physiological, historical, social or environmental aspects of worry, but that it sees them all as part of a spiritual issue—that worry, ultimately, is a response to life lived in God's world. Worry is, therefore, a response to God himself.

The challenge when we try to define worry is this: to avoid over-simplistic, trite definitions that don't go deep enough, and trite answers that don't take account of our very real struggles. Ultimately, the Bible calls us to honestly face the problem and all of the suffering while offering real hope that goes deep to the heart of the person struggling with worry.

Once you understand how the Bible defines worry, you are more able to understand and appreciate how Scripture talks about it. The Bible is very insightful in helping us think about what worry is and why we feel it. Let's take another look at Jesus' teaching in Matthew 6 v 25-34, and consider the specific word that is translated "worry" in our English Bibles:

Therefore I tell you, do not worry about your life, what you will eat or drink; or about your body, what you will wear. Is not life more than food, and the body more than clothes? Look at the birds of the air; they do not sow or reap or store away in barns, and yet your heavenly Father feeds them. Are you not much more valuable than they? Can any one of you by worrying add a single hour to your life?

And why do you worry about clothes? See how the flowers of the field grow. They do not labor or spin. Yet I tell you that not even Solomon in all his splendor was dressed like one of these. If that is how God clothes the grass of the field, which is here today and tomorrow is thrown into the fire, will he not much more clothe you—you of little faith? So do not worry, saying, "What shall we eat?" or "What shall we drink?" or "What shall we wear?" For the pagans run after all these things, and your heavenly Father knows that you need them. But seek first his kingdom and his righteousness, and all these things will be given to you as well. Therefore do not worry about tomorrow, for tomorrow will worry about itself. Each day has enough trouble of its own.

Five times, Jesus uses the word "worry". Three times, it's a command. And the Greek word used in the Gospel is *merimnao*. It literally means "a distracted mind" or a "double mind." In the broader context of the passage, this division, or divided loyalty, is between the kingdom of God and my own kingdom. It is to be distracted from the first kingdom by the other. The Bible scholar Dick France has a really helpful insight into what worry therefore is: *it is to be over-concerned about something other than the kingdom of God.*

That is what worry is: over-concern. This is quite simple, and hugely helpful. It is also helpful in telling us what worry is not.

1. Worry is not the Same as Concern

If worry is "over-concern," then it is different from "concern". It is appropriate to be concerned about things. What Jesus is forbidding is "over-concern," and not concern, itself.

When my oldest child was beginning to drive, I had legitimate concerns, because I was well aware of how dangerous driving could be if not properly prepared. So I acted as any responsible parent would; I made sure she received appropriate driver training (I was wise enough to get a professional and not take on the task myself!). And I prayed for her (and for the other road users!).

That was godly concern. It leads to wise action and dependent prayer. Similarly, this is why I lock my doors to my house when I am away or during the night and pray that God will keep the place safe. There are many other examples from our daily lives which can flow from proper, godly concern: regular doctor checkups, balancing your finances, preparing for a child's college education, getting your car serviced regularly. Jesus is not telling us not to be concerned about things. He is telling us not to be over-concerned. The two are not the same, and you can recognize the difference because concern takes wise action and prays dependently. Worry, or over-concern, thinks and acts as though everything is up to you, or completely out of control, and prays desperately, if at all.

2. The Solution to Worry is not Becoming Laid-back

The answer to "over-concern" is not "under-concern." The antidote to "over-concern" is not just being a lazy or "laid-back" person. Often times, being disengaged and indifferent can masquerade as godliness when in fact it is not. We all know laid-back people. Maybe you are one yourself. It can seem a wonderful way to live! But it is worth digging below the laid-back surface. Consider these three very different "laid back" people:

1. First, a person who is laid-back on the outside can still be a deeply worried person on the inside. They mask their anxiety by acting cool and collected. People like this tend to be driven, prickly and overly sensitive.

2. Second, a laid-back person can also be a deep worrier but one who has chosen to disengage and become indifferent. These kinds of worriers tend to be procrastinators. They avoid life.

3. Finally, someone can seem very calm and laid-back, but in fact they are deeply engaged with and invested in others' lives and situations. They care deeply and passionately; and they are taking their worries to God and depending upon him as they face life's challenges.

Those are three very different ways to be "laid-back." The first two are not the answer to worry; and the third is not laid-back so much as God-dependent.

3. Work is not Necessarily an Expression of Worry

Another common error is to think that the way to avoid worry is to become passive, and simply look to God to provide for all of your needs. Jesus' illustrations about birds and plants might seem to suggest that passivity is next to godliness! Nothing could be further from the truth. God may provide food for the birds, but they have to actively go and get it. Plants do not automatically grow; they must draw on the nutrients in the soil and sun. So working hard is not necessarily (or even often) an expression of worry. In fact, it is a virtue. In 1 Thessalonians 4 v 11-12, Paul says:

> Make it your ambition to lead a quiet life: you should mind your own business and work with your hands, just as we told you, so that your daily life may win the respect of outsiders and so that you will not be dependent on anybody.

And he warns in 2 Thessalonians 3:10: "The one who is unwilling to work shall not eat." You can't get more straightforward than that! So clearly, Jesus is not saying that we are to stop all activities and sit idly by while life happens around us. Of course, working extremely hard could be a sign that we are deeply, chronically over-concerned; but it is not automatically so.

4. Protecting Yourself is not the Same as Worry

It is important to understand that godly fear and concern for your safety and the safety of others is *not* the same as the "worry" that Jesus is commanding us to avoid.

Suppose that you are driving on a highway at night and you see another car heading toward you. A godly response would be to do whatever you can to steer your car to avoid an accident. Or suppose you are currently fearful for your own safety, or the safety of another person, because you have reason to believe that someone is going to harm you or them. You would be completely justified in doing whatever you can to protect yourself and others from harm. We read in the Gospels of how Jesus himself avoided the crowds who wanted to harm him because he knew he had more work and ministry to do (Luke 4 v 28-30). If you are reading this book and you are in a situation where you might be abused or harmed, then take action now to protect yourself. Call a friend or a pastor. If you are being threatened by your spouse, a parent, or anyone else, it would be wise and loving to contact an abuse center or the police. That is an expression of godly concern. I want to say as strongly as I can: it is not wrong to take action and seek help if you're suffering, or fearing, abuse of any kind.

This World, or God's Kingdom?

With these four caveats in place, let's return to what worry *is*. The broader context of Matthew 6 v 25-34 brings clarity to the essence of worry. Jesus' teaching on worry comes in his famous "Sermon on the Mount," where he outlines how members of God's kingdom—those who enjoy following and trusting him as their King—will live. Each of the sections that come before the one we're looking at in this chapter emphasize the priority of a kingdom orientation over an "earthly" one; each compares living life for the here and now with living for something much bigger—something eternal. The challenge Jesus is repeatedly posing is: *Are you living as if this life is all there is, or are you living your life for the kingdom of God?*

- Are you giving to the needy to be seen by others now, or to serve the kingdom and please your Father (6 v 1-4)?
- Are you praying to impress others, or to further the work of the kingdom and relate to your heavenly Father (v 5-15)?

- Are you fasting so others notice, or to serve your Father (v 16-18)?
- Are you storing up treasures in this temporary life, or in the next, eternal one (v 19-24)?

Kingdom giving means doing good deeds not for the praise of man, but of God. Kingdom prayer means that we pray as children of the Father, who we trust for our every provision. Kingdom fasting means to choose personal sacrifice before the eyes of God and not man. Kingdom treasure in heaven means we are ultimately living for something bigger than the here and now.

In each of these examples, the distinction is between living for something in creation (the praise and recognition of other humans) or living for the Creator (his recognition and praise). And so it's natural that Jesus turns next to his command not to worry. Worry begins when a person is trying to love equally both the Creator and something in creation (or when they are not trying to love the Creator at all, having replaced him with something in his creation). That something may be ourselves, of course. And to love Creator and created equally is impossible. Matthew 6 v 24 captures the entire section well:

> No one can serve two masters. Either you will hate the one and love the other, or you will be devoted to the one and despise the other. You cannot serve both God and Money.

Which God?

The essence of worry is in attempting to find your ultimate hope, comfort and meaning in something that is temporal and fleeting. It happens when you treat something in creation as a "god"—so you rely on it, and seek blessing in it. When you do that, you have set yourself up for worry, because nothing in creation lasts and nothing in creation has everything under control (including you!). This world lacks the stability you need in order to be worry free. If you put your hope in things that are unstable, you will be unstable. Your loyalty is divided between something in creation (money is just one example) and God. Something in creation (even a good thing) is usurping the rightful place that only God deserves in your life. Whenever you place your ultimate hope in anything in this world, you will struggle with worry. The more you do this, the more pronounced your struggle will be.

Every moment of every day, we are making choices about what is most important in life. While theoretically we may say that God is most important in our lives, and we may say we know that he is in control, we struggle to live this way practically in light of the circumstances we face on a regular basis.

In other words, worry is over-concern that results from "over-loving" something—that is, loving it more than God. Concern results when you love something in a proper way and not more than God. Indifference is a lack of love. It is the opposite of worry, not the antidote or cure for worry.

A Worrying Spectrum

The causes of worry are as numerous as the circumstances of our lives. And the amount, and manner, of our worrying will also be shaped by our character. Some of us are more naturally worriers; others are naturally more indifferent. So depending on who you are, and what your life is currently like, this book will speak in a different way to you than your neighbor or friend from church. So let's plot out on a spectrum what we are talking about:

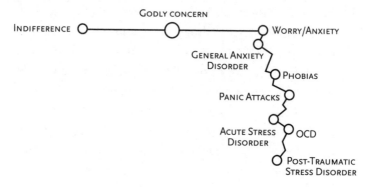

- *Concern:* Being concerned about something is not wrong in itself. There are many things that you should be concerned about and responsibly use your gifts and abilities to address. Scripture does not teach you to live a passive life as if your actions don't matter.
- *Worry:* When you move beyond concern you enter into all of the different varieties and degrees of worry or anxiety; worry and anxiety are the same thing.

As the intensity of anxiety increases, it becomes more life-dominating and debilitating to the person and their relationships. Psychologists have developed psychiatric labels to try to define the different levels of anxiety. These labels capture the experience of worry and its potential impact on someone's life and relationships. The following terms are becoming more common in our daily conversations:

- General Anxiety Disorder (GAD)
- Phobias: anxiety with an object. Fear of flying, crowds, public speaking, spiders, etc.
- Panic Attacks

- Obsessive/Compulsive Disorder (OCD)
- Acute Stress Disorder
- Post-Traumatic Stress Disorder (PTSD)

All of these struggles are forms of suffering that should be taken seriously, regardless of the label that is attached to them. Often, when worry expresses itself in these more intense ways, typically there are historical issues in your past that may be impacting you today. In addition, anxiety at these levels may also include a physiological component (racing heartbeat, struggle to breathe, etc.). When this is the case, it may be more challenging to grow and change; but it does not mean that you can't. While worry is fundamentally a matter of the soul, it does not mean that you should minimize these other important layers that may make your struggle with anxiety more acute and life-dominating; but it also does not mean that the truths of Scripture do not apply or cannot help. These are all different degrees of the same thing: anxiety or worry. So be encouraged; in whatever way you struggle, God has something to say to you in his word.

What About Fear?

There is one more word associated with this whole area: fear. To fear something (or someone) is to be in awe of it, so that it directs your emotions and behavior. Fear is usually a bad thing; but the Bible uses it positively when God is the One we fear. Why? Because it is a good thing to be in awe of God, to recognize who he is and relate to him in a way that changes how we feel and act. So King Solomon wrote that:

> The fear of the LORD is the beginning of knowledge.
>
> (Proverbs 1 v 7)

And the writer of Psalm 130 sang:

> With you there is forgiveness; therefore you are feared.
>
> (v 4, NIV84)

When we understand the majesty and the grace of the creating, saving God, we are in awe of him, and that is reflected in how we live. That is a right fear, because God deserves all our awe. To fear anything else is to make it a "god" in our lives.

In the same way that the Bible commands us not to worry or be anxious, it also calls us to not be afraid or be fearful in an ungodly way. Instead, we are to rightly fear God or be in awe of him because he is awesome, great, gracious and powerful. In fact, when you fear God in this way, it will enable you to face all of your fears, anxieties and worries in new and liberating ways.

Spotting Our Over-loves

Let's begin to ask the question: "What do *you* tend to worry about?" If worry is caused by over-loving something, so that you become over-concerned about having it, increasing it, or keeping it, where do you see that happening in your own life? Worry is a sign that you have made something other than God your functional god. It is the same for all of us. So let's get very practical and consider the following good things that can become your god:

- **Your job:** If your job is what you over-love as your ultimate provider or worth-giver, you'll be over-concerned. If you make your job more important than God, you will worry about your performance and be overwhelmed at the thought of losing your job or not getting the recognition you desire.

- **Your spouse:** If your husband or wife is where you turn first and foremost to know love, you'll be over-concerned about your marriage. You will worry about being let down or possibly rejected by your spouse because your expectations of your spouse, or of yourself as a spouse, will far outweigh what either of you can ever deliver.

- **Your reputation:** If you over-love others' opinion of you, finding your value in their appraisal, you will be over-concerned about it. If you make your reputation more important than God, you will worry about making a mistake or doing something foolish. You may find yourself trying to impress people all of the time, or struggling with defensiveness when questioned.

- **Your children:** If your children are the place where you find your sense of purpose or significance, you are loving them too much. If you make your children and how they turn out more important to you than God, you will worry about every decision they make. You will likely be an overly vigilant or critical parent.

- **Your moral record:** If you place your confidence about your eternal destination in your moral record, you will be hugely over-concerned about your performance. You may possibly minimize your failures, make excuses for yourself or become judgmental of others to make you feel better about your own record.

No matter what you over-love, whenever you make the blessing more important than the Giver of the blessing, you will be anxious and, ironically, you will likely do harm to that blessing.

Worry: An Opportunity

How can worry be an opportunity? When you find yourself worrying, you actually have an opportunity to see what kinds of things tend to get your attention more than God. Your over-concerns reveal your over-loves. This can be an opportunity to grow.

I am someone who can over-love order because it provides me with a sense of control and comfort. When my ordering of my world becomes an over-concern, I tend to become bossy with others or impatient. As I write this chapter, I am at a coffee shop due to a ferocious winter storm that came through the area where I live. We lost power on Tuesday and it has not been restored yet. Today is Friday. I am living within circumstances that are threatening my ability to control my world. In addition, our house is without heat, thus threatening my comfort.

How will I choose to respond? Will I be indifferent, and let my wife sort the house out (and my publisher cope with my missed deadline!)? Will I be anxious, on edge and impatient with my family and the power company? Will I focus on my own problems, or will I check on and serve my neighbors? To put it concisely, will I love God most, letting him be in control and seeking comfort in knowing him, or will I over-love having electricity?

Ironically, when God is more important to me than an aspect of this world, I will be more useful to myself and others in handling or caring for that aspect. Having a soul that is riveted on God's glory does not make me less useful here and now, but more useful. We tend to think that the way to be most useful is to fixate on our present circumstances; in fact, focusing on God frees us truly to live wisely and lovingly in those circumstances. Living a kingdom lifestyle seems upside down, but it is really right side up.

It is important to see that you are making these kinds of choices all the time. They may seem like mundane matters, but they are terribly important. Our lives can be shaped by some unique, traumatic and monumental moment, but for most of us, our lives are molded far more by daily decisions and reactions over a long period of time. Matters of character are forged over the long haul. If I am not vigilant about my growth in grace on a daily basis, I will not be prepared when the bigger challenges in life arise.

So What is the Cure for Worry?

The rest of this book will address and answer this question! But let's begin to deal with our worries by looking at one reason Jesus provides for not worrying in Matthew 5 v 33, in the heart of the passage we've been looking at. It is precisely what we have been discussing already. Jesus has a way of cutting to the core of the problem and providing a deeper, more substantial solution:

> But seek first his kingdom and his righteousness, and all these things will be given to you as well.

Jesus is bringing us back to the right priorities. *What are you living for?* he asks. He is calling us to re-orient our lives around the living God and his priorities. He knows that, as long as we live for secondary things and not for him, we will be fraught with over-concerns. Anxiety will be our normal existence, because anything that is not connected to the kingdom of God and his righteousness is fleeting. The apostle Peter, quoting Isaiah 40 v 6-8, says this about this present age:

All people are like grass, and all their glory is like the
flowers of the field; the grass withers and the flowers fall,
but the word of the Lord endures forever. (1 Peter 1 v 24-25)

We need to keep first things first and second things second.
We are to prioritize the kingdom, by viewing everything
through the lens of our faith. We need to see our past, our
future and our present in terms of the truths of the gospel. It's
to those three viewpoints that we now turn.

Questions for Reflection

1. If you had a minute to explain to someone what worry
   is, what would you say?
2. What is your pattern when you worry? Do you tend to
   disengage or become hyper-vigilant?
3. Since there is a fine line between concern and over-
   concern, what types of behaviors help you see when
   you have moved from one to the other?
4. Can you see how your worries do, or could, reveal
   your over-loves?
5. Is there someone you can ask to pray for you as you
   read this book?

3. Worry and your Past (Part One)

When it comes to dirt, there is always something.

Robert Penn Warren was a great American novelist from the Deep South. In his greatest novel, *All the King's Men*, the corrupt Governor of Louisiana, Willie Stark, asks his friend, political journalist Jack Burden, to find some "dirt" from his rival's past. Burden says that, when it comes to this particular political enemy, he'll not be able to find anything, to which Stark confidently replies:

> *"Man is conceived in sin and born in corruption and he passeth from the stink of the didie [ie: diaper; nappy] to the stench of the shroud. There is always something."*

As Stark knew so well, there is dirt, flaws, sin, in everyone's past. There is always something. The question we face is not: *Is it there?* but: *What will you do about it?* While the Bible never dismisses our suffering, it aims to deal with our most fundamental need: forgiveness and cleansing of our own sins and failures. We will deal with past suffering in the next chapter; in this one, we focus on that most central need.

Facing my Dirt

When I was seventeen, and before I became a Christian, something began to happen to me. The dirty "somethings" of my past began to emerge—not in public, but in my heart. My conscience started working overtime. One day life was going along just fine... then it came to a screeching halt. I had no idea what caused the change (now I know that it was simply that the Holy Spirit had begun to work in me). I was weighed down by so much guilt. It was as if my past actions became actual people before whom I stood, facing the weight and shame of their accusations. I found myself in a courtroom, where countless witnesses took the stand and began to reveal all of my misdeeds, failures, weaknesses and sins. It was almost unbearable.

And what made it worse was when some people I knew talked to me about "knowing Jesus." That reminded me that I didn't know him! I knew he was called a Savior, but I knew he wasn't mine. I knew he was called the Son of God, and I knew I had no relationship to God. So when I was around people who had these things sorted out, I struggled to like them... yet at the same time, I was drawn to them. In the midst of this crisis, I felt as if worry and fear had me in their grasp. I was overcome with a sense of brokenness within. I felt the disjointedness around me. The people in my life, the world around me and the entire cosmos seemed out of kilter.

In keeping with Willie Stark's assessment of human nature, I was facing my "dirt" and it was being used against me by myself. The bare, brute fact of the reality of my sin had come crashing down upon me like a ton of bricks. I was experiencing what modern thinkers call an "existential crisis." Many years later, I realized that I was going through what Soren Kierkegaard and the modern existentialists attempted to explain with the word "angst." "Angst" is originally a Dutch and German word that describes an intense feeling of apprehension, anxiety or inner turmoil. Perhaps the English word "dread" comes close to capturing it. It captures the sense that we live in a disjointed universe as individuals who are disjointed from ourselves, others, the entire cosmos and, ultimately, God. While the modern existentialists captured our experience of angst, most did not connect the separation to our sinful state of being alienated from God. That is where Scripture goes much deeper in terms of the cause of our alienation.

Have you ever felt this way? Is this something that you are struggling with right now? If so, how have you attempted to deal with it so far—and has what you have tried helped?

Woe to Me!

As I read the Bible, I realized that it captured this disorientation better than any other books I had read in literature or philosophy. In fact, the Bible helped me to see that things were worse than I had originally thought. It also provided hope that I had not yet considered. Two passages that resonated with me were Isaiah 6 and Jonah 2. Here is how Isaiah describes his experience as he comes to terms with his sin and uncleanness;

> In the year that King Uzziah died, I saw the Lord, high and exalted, seated on a throne; and the train of his robe filled the temple. Above him were seraphim, each with six wings: With two wings they covered their faces, with two they covered their feet, and with two they were flying. And they were calling to one another:
>
> "Holy, holy, holy is the LORD Almighty;
>   the whole earth is full of his glory."
>
> At the sound of their voices the doorposts and thresholds shook and the temple was filled with smoke.

> "Woe to me!" I cried. "I am ruined! For I am a man of
> unclean lips, and I live among a people of unclean lips,
> and my eyes have seen the King, the LORD Almighty."
>
> (Isaiah 6 v 1-5)

As Isaiah stands in the presence of the Holy One of Israel, all
he can say is: "Woe to me." This cry is one of utter fear and
abandonment. He is "ruined." The root of this word means "to
be silent," and is associated with the silence that accompanies
death. Isaiah is literally saying: *I have been made to cease, I am cut
off, undone, doomed to die.* Isaiah expresses more fully and ably
what the 20th-century existentialists were grasping to describe.
For the modern existentialist, humanity is alone in the universe.
Life is meaningless. Humanity is a freak of nature, looking for
meaning when there is none. But for Isaiah, it is actually even
worse than that. He stands before the real, personal God, whose
holiness means that Isaiah no longer exists. He is not just alone;
it is as though he were literally dead. His problem is not a cold,
merciless universe. It is the living, perfect God.

In *Isaiah: God Saves Sinners,* Ray Ortlund quotes from John
Oswalt's *The Book of Isaiah, Chapters 1 – 39* and then comments:

> "'Such confrontation cannot help but produce despair. For
> the finite, the mortal, the incomplete, and the fallible to
> encounter the Infinite, the Eternal, the Self-consistent, and
> the Infallible is to know the futility and the hopelessness of
> one's existence.' ... It is not the recognition of his finitude
> which crushes Isaiah; it is his uncleanness. The primary
> element about God's holiness that distinguishes him from
> human beings is not his essence but his character ... Isaiah
> recognizes with sickening force that his character is not, any
> more than is his people's, in keeping with God's character."

Isaiah is "undone," because he is unclean. He is a prophet, giving his life up in service of God. But even for him, there is sin. There is always something.

While my experience was not the same as Isaiah's by degree, it was the same in kind. I was coming to grips with my finitude; but even more, I was coming to grips with my sin. A deep and abiding angst was present. The knowledge and weight of past sins and failures were beginning to make me sink.

Running from God

My experience was captured in a different way by another prophet, named Jonah. Jonah is given the task to go and preach repentance and forgiveness of sins to a group of people he despises. They are enemies of his own people. In response to this clear call from God, Jonah proceeds literally to run in the opposite direction from the one in which God has commanded him to go. Jonah's actions are symbolic of his attitude. All disobedience is the exact opposite of obedience. There are no shades of gray between obedience and disobedience.

This is what I was coming to grips with. I had thought that I had done a fairly good job of being a civil, relatively obedient child and citizen. Ultimately though, these things were all convincing me that I did not need God! I was running away from God by thinking I did not need him.

In his mercy, God brought Jonah to his knees, in the belly of a fish. Hear what Jonah says in his state of despair as he awakens to his own need of God.

> In my distress I called to the LORD,
>   and he answered me.
> From deep in the realm of the dead I called for help,
>   and you listened to my cry.

You hurled me into the depths,

   into the very heart of the seas,

   and the currents swirled about me;

all your waves and breakers

   swept over me.

I said, "I have been banished

   from your sight;

yet I will look again

   toward your holy temple."

The engulfing waters threatened me,

   the deep surrounded me;

   seaweed was wrapped around my head.

To the roots of the mountains I sank down;

   the earth beneath barred me in forever. (Jonah 2 v 2-6)

If Isaiah represents what it is like to see your sin in stark contrast to God's utter perfection, Jonah captures the experience of how your sin separates you from God, and actually propels you to run away from him and his presence. Isaiah experiences death and Jonah experiences a vast separation as he faces his dirt and sinks to the very depths of the ocean.

How Jesus Deals with Angst

Have you ever experienced a degree of this "angst"? If you have, at one level that is a good thing. It is only when we are deeply concerned about our past sins and their implication for our relationship with God that we are aware of our need of God's forgiving grace. Godly concern—in this case, God-wrought angst—leads to wise action and dependent prayer. But when it comes to our uncleanness, the action is God's, and wisdom is simply to accept his act. For Isaiah, God acted to send an angel bringing a coal to cleanse his lips by fire. The fire of God's presence brings judgment, but also brings cleansing. When Jesus arrives on the scene, John the Baptist says of him:

> He will baptize you with the Holy Spirit and fire. His winnowing fork is in his hand, and he will clear his threshing floor, gathering his wheat into the barn and burning up the chaff with unquenchable fire.
>
> (Matthew 3 v 11-12)

Jesus comes both to consume and purify: to judge and to save. How can the unclean be made clean? How can the impure stand pure before God? It is only in seeing and accepting the fact that when Jesus was on the cross, he experienced God's consuming fire of judgment in your place. The utterly pure Son of God took the place of the impure; of you and me. Because he stood in your place, you can stand before God, forgiven, clean and pure. Like Isaiah's, your past sins can be forgiven, due to the fact that Jesus was "scorched to death" by God's unquenchable, consuming fire. Because he suffered this, you can now experience his cleansing fire; the power and presence of the Holy Spirit in you, enabling you to face your worries.

To think of this another way, consider the story of Jonah. As Jonah was, Jesus was "thrown overboard"—but he was separated from his Father not because of his dirt, but because of ours. When Jonah disobeyed, God sent a storm that saw him thrown out of his escape boat and sinking beneath the waves, drowning, before God sent the fish to rescue him from death. It may seem like a stretch to connect Jonah's experience with that of Jesus; except that Jesus himself does this in Matthew 12 v 39-41:

> A wicked and adulterous generation asks for a sign! But none will be given it except the sign of the prophet Jonah. For as Jonah was three days and three nights in

the belly of a huge fish, so the Son of Man will be three days and three nights in the heart of the earth. The men of Nineveh will stand up at the judgment with this generation and condemn it; for they repented at the preaching of Jonah, and now something greater than Jonah is here.

Do you see the parallel again? Jonah's experience is pointing to Jesus' death, burial and resurrection. Jonah sank because of his own disobedience, and was spared death. Jesus sank because of our disobedience, right down into the grave. And yet Jesus was raised up from that grave, as Jonah was from the fish; and through faith, we are raised in him (Ephesians 2 v 4-8).

It is only as we feel the weight of our past sins—only as we feel angst at who we are and what we have done—that we are able to take that burden to the cross and appreciate what it means for Jesus to bear our sins for us. Looking back, I can see that God's Spirit was convicting me of my uncleanness and separation from God in order to point me to the cross and his grace.

John Newton was a pastor and hymn writer. One of his most famous hymns was *Amazing Grace*. Many people remember the first verse, but few know the second. Newton captures the dual work of the Spirit when using guilt-produced angst to save someone from themselves:

"Twas grace that taught my heart to fear,
and grace my fears relieved;
how precious did that grace appear
the hour I first believed!"

The gospel tells us that we should fear, because we are sinners. But the gospel also relieves our fear and removes our angst, because it tells us that there is a place where our sins can be fully and finally dealt with.

Taking your Past to Jesus

What does this mean? It means that if you are not a Christian—not someone who has ever truly asked Jesus, the Son of God, to take your sins, bear your judgment and experience your separation—then you should feel very fearful about your past sins. Everyone has dirt. There is always something; in fact, there are always many things, because everyone has disobeyed God. Do not belittle, excuse or try to ignore your sin. Jonah found that did not work.

Admit the reality. Feel the angst. And then know that while you should be deeply fearful, you do not need to be! Jesus has paid for your sins and you don't have to. Feel angst over past sins, and then let it lead you to Christ. A great Christian author, John Stott, once said that there is nothing wrong with shame and guilt—as long as they lead you to Christ!

If you are a Christian, do you still worry about past sins? Maybe you acknowledge God's cleansing grace for you in Christ, but you still see the consequences of past sins in the present. If so, the consequences are a reality and should serve as a reminder of the ripple effect of disobedience. But rather than that leading you to anxiety, it should lead to greater resolve to make every effort to flee sin and embrace obedience. But don't forget that you have been forgiven of your past sins. God will not stand in judgment over you due to the fact that Jesus has borne his judgment for you, in your place as your substitute.

If you are worried about your past sins, then this is "over-concern." Why? Because Jesus has taken those sins from you. It may be a sign that, deep down, you think you need to make yourself loveable to God before he will love you; you think you need to earn his acceptance. You are over-loving your own obedience. And this will cause you to run from God completely or live in great anxiety about his opinion of you. Every day becomes another day to run further away or try harder to keep God's judgment far away. No one can bear to live life with that kind of load upon them. You are living with only half of the story. You are knowing the "woe"; but now you need to see that Jesus took that woe away from you, dealt with it, and now you are free to live as a beloved child of God. Our angst over our sin should always drive us to the cross, rather than to worry.

God's Voice is Loudest

Are you someone whose worries are caused by, or increased by, events and actions in your past, whether committed by you or against you? Each of us has a history that is utterly unique; but many of us worry about our past sins and failures, or about past sins that have been committed against us. Because of the past, we worry about the present. We can't seem to move on from what we were, or what we did, or what was done to us (read the next chapter for more on dealing with things that have been done to us).

You may feel deep shame for something you have done, or something done to you. The guilt and sense of unworthiness has rendered you almost dead or thrown you into a sinking spiral, falling further and further away from the joy of knowing and serving God. If that's you, then right now, as you read, is the time to remember God's saving mercies; to look at your past sins and failures and see that they do not define you. Yes, the consequences may never go away, and you may continue to struggle with them, but they do not and can never speak words about you or over you that are louder than the voice of God; and he declares that you are forgiven and cleansed and loved in Christ. If you are a Christian, then whatever else has happened, the most important event "in your past" is the cross.

The Problem with Nearsightedness

You will need to come to the cross daily, because in twenty-four hours today will be yesterday. The sins committed today are the potential guilt and anxiety of tomorrow. Feeling the reality of past sins and then fighting against worrying about them is a daily calling.

The apostle Paul experienced this in Romans 7, where he speaks about his own ongoing inner turmoil. He finds that he does things he shouldn't do and fails to do things he should do:

> I do not understand what I do. For what I want to do I do
> not do, but what I hate I do.   (Romans 7 v 15)

What does he do with this? He tells himself (and his readers):

> Thanks be to God, who delivers me through Jesus Christ
> our Lord ... there is now no condemnation for those who
> are in Christ Jesus.   (7 v 25; 8 v 1)

It seems to me that Paul echoes the tension of the daily life of the believer. Romans 7 v 15 and 8 v 1 are simultaneously true of any Christian. Keeping these together is the only way to remain realistic, sane and peaceful. You can be honest about the struggle rather than deny it, hide it or play it down. But you can remain optimistic because at the very same time that Romans 7 v 15 is true, so is Romans 8 v 1.

The apostle Peter knew this all too well. He knew that guilt and worry over past sins would render Christians impotent to make progress in their lives. He calls his readers to pursue goodness, knowledge, self-control, perseverance, godliness, mutual affection and love, all built on and springing from faith in God's promises. Why? Because:

> ... if you possess these qualities in increasing measure, they will keep you from being ineffective and unproductive in your knowledge of our Lord Jesus Christ. But whoever does not have them is nearsighted and blind, forgetting that they have been cleansed from their past sins. (2 Peter 1 v 8-9)

Do you see Peter's point? It is possible to forget that you have been cleansed from sins, and to see only past sins. It is possible to forget that there is now *no* condemnation for those who are in Christ Jesus. We can become nearsighted (or what British people call "shortsighted"), so that we can only see what is up close and obvious: our failures, shortcomings and sins. That makes us unproductive, stuck, full of anxiety rather than hope. If you have ever thought that you cannot be useful to Christ because of what you've done (or what you've done again), this is what was happening; you were suffering nearsightedness. You must become farsighted and focus not only on the truth of Romans 7 v 15, but on the great and overpowering reality of Romans 8 v 1. Your past sins have been forgiven. You are not, and can never be, condemned for them.

I have done a great deal of pastoral counseling over the past 25 – 30 years. Often, I would counsel someone who was stuck and could not seem to make any progress in their Christian growth. Inevitably, as we would meet, we would stumble upon a past sin, a pattern of sin or some deeply shaming experience that resembled a big log lodged in a cog of a grist mill. The mill was at a standstill, because the log would keep the gears from moving. It would take some patience and time to locate the log of sin or experience of shame that had become lodged in the person's heart. It would take even longer to see how the grace of the gospel was the only hope of getting the sin and shame dislodged.

Now No Condemnation

Do you struggle with worry and anxiety that is connected to past failures and sins? If so, have you identified them; and are you more focused on them than on Christ? If so, look upward and outward to Christ. If you find that you are having a hard time doing that, ask someone or a group of people to help you and to pray for and with you. Let me encourage you to cry out to God for grace to give you a fresh understanding, in your heart as much as in your head, of his grace for you. Don't let your nearsightedness keep your gaze fixed solely upon Romans 7 v 15. Pray for farsightedness, for Romans 8 v 1 to take root more deeply in your heart.

When you feel angst over your sin, remember that this is a world in which Jesus died for sin. Do not allow yourself to bear the burden of anxiety that our uncleanness and separation brings. Say to yourself: *There is now no condemnation for me because I am in Christ Jesus. There is now no need to be anxious about what I have done, because this is a world where my God died on a cross. Jesus took my burden, my shame and my angst on the cross.* Once you have reminded yourself of these truths, talk to God and thank him for his redeeming grace. Ask him to help you move forward upon this foundation of grace.

Questions For Reflection

1. What specific things about your past cause you to worry the most? Are they sins that you have committed or something traumatic that has happened to you?

2. How does the experience of Isaiah or Jonah resonate with you?

3. Do you see that worry or fear over your past sins can be a good thing if it leads you to God for grace and mercy?

4. Have you ever brought your sins to the cross and come to personal faith in Christ? If not, will you do so now?

5. If you have, then are there areas where you are being nearsighted? What would it look like to keep the cross in focus?

4. Worry and your Past (Part Two)

Cynthia grew up in an abusive home. When she was in her early teens, she was verbally and emotionally abused by both her parents. At some point, she was also sexually molested. Now she is in her thirties and she has battled with anxiety for years. In addition, she has battled with other things like depression, panic attacks, eating disorders, self-harm and suicidal thoughts. She struggles to sleep at night and she has frequent nightmares.

Tom grew up in a military family. He moved every three or four years and often found himself feeling like the new kid on the block. On a couple of occasions, Tom moved to a new place only to experience horrible bullying. Even now, as an adult, Tom tends to be more anxious in his relationships due to those experiences. Now he is in his forties and he finds that he does not like to be alone in crowds. He can also become very anxious whenever he feels like there is tension between him and someone else, which has caused difficulties in his marriage and at work, because when it happens, he will either run or fight.

Jonathan grew up in a very normal home. His parents loved him and he had lots of friends. He was just a "normal" young boy who enjoyed an uneventful childhood. This changed in a split second, when he witnessed a terrible car accident in which several people were killed. He had a very close view of what happened. The images in the past seem to have a life of their own in the present. They jump into his head without any warning, and he feels as though he's back in that moment.

Susan was a devout Christian and enjoyed working as a volunteer in a ministry with other friends and fellow Christians. Through a confusing turn of events, her character was attacked, horrible things were said about her, and she was told she could no longer be part of the ministry. Years later, she still struggles to go to church or do anything that reminds her of what happened to her. She has found it particularly difficult to have annual job evaluations and deals with deep anxiety for several weeks before she meets with her work supervisor.

Triggers

You may have read the last chapter and found it did not quite do what you were needing—because it is not so much past sins that cause you anxiety in the present, but past experiences that you contributed nothing to, but were a victim of. You may have identified deeply or in part with the people I began this chapter with (who are not real people, but are based on people I know). Or you may have a different anxiety-inducing story from your past that we could have added to this chapter's opening. And if you don't struggle with the past in this way, there is a high chance that someone you live with or know well does.

When you have experienced varying degrees of trauma in your past, the memories of the event or events can live on in the present. Usually, this happens through what are known as "triggers": things that remind you of the past event and bring the anxiety and fear associated with that event into the present. For Cynthia, it could be a family photo, a smell, or returning home to visit family where the abuse occurred.

Jonathan would have a hard time watching the morning news whenever the morning commute, traffic and current accidents are discussed. Tom will become anxious whenever he finds himself in a situation where he feels attacked or criticized by someone. Susan feels anxious whenever she finds herself asked to sing one of the hymns that were the favorites of the group she was a part of.

What are your triggers? It is good to know the kinds of things that can provoke you to becoming anxious in the present due to an experience in the past. But you not only want to know what your triggers are; you also want to know what to do when the anxiety rushes at you.

Suffering and the God of the Bible

An entire book could be written on this aspect of anxiety. (In fact, I wrote a shorter book on the subject where I focused on the experience of post-traumatic stress disorder, called *PTSD: Healing for Bad Memories*.) When current anxiety is connected to aspects of our past, it often does make the struggle with worry more difficult and pronounced. If there are historical, relational and physiological aspects intertwined with anxiety in the present, the fight will be harder. That does not mean that the God of the Bible is somehow out of his league in terms of providing deep comfort and enabling grace to grow and change.

There are two dangers to avoid when dealing with any struggle. The first is being simplistic when describing worry caused by past events. Each and every person is unique and complex. To pigeonhole every person who struggles with worry is to fail to appreciate this complexity. A second danger is to give the impression that there are some "pathological" struggles that the Bible is not capable of addressing because it was written at a time before the advent of modern psychology and psychiatry. While there can be much to glean from these disciplines, they still do not address the core of worry at the level of Scripture. It is worth remembering that our most basic problem, whether we feel it or not, is our rebellion against God—that we are sinners who need forgiveness. And so it is worth appreciating that God has already addressed this in Jesus' life, death and resurrection—through faith in him, we are forgiven sinners. That is what we talked about in the previous chapter, and it is worth reminding yourself of it throughout this chapter.

But we also know that God is very concerned about the suffering we experience. Though the Bible does not give us an exhaustive answer to the origin of evil and suffering, it provides one of the most robust solutions to the problem. At the very center of the Bible is the God who became man to forgive and free people at great cost to himself. Paul's description of Jesus in Philippians 2 v 6-8 captures this wonderfully:

> Who, being in very nature God,
>> did not consider equality with God something to be used
>> to his own advantage;
> rather, he made himself nothing
>> by taking the very nature of a servant,
>> being made in human likeness.
> And being found in appearance as a man,
>> he humbled himself
>> by becoming obedient to death—
>>> even death on a cross!

So in Jesus, we discover a God who identifies with our suffering because he has suffered, too:

In bringing many sons and daughters to glory, it was fitting that God, for whom and through whom everything exists, should make the pioneer of their salvation perfect through what he suffered.

Since the children have flesh and blood, he too shared in their humanity so that by his death he might break the power of him who holds the power of death—that is, the devil—and free those who all their lives were held in slavery by their fear of death. For surely it is not angels he helps, but Abraham's descendants. For this reason he had to be made like them, fully human in every way ... Because he himself suffered when he was tempted, he is able to help those who are being tempted.

(Hebrews 2 v 10, 14-17, 18)

If you have suffered, this is the God you want to be close to, and the God you want to be close to you. He knows. He cares. He understands.

Transforming Memories

You cannot change your past, neither what has been done to you or what has happened to you. What you can do is begin to work out how to live now in a way that is not in the grip of those things. And that involves working out how to live life in a way that lets God be in charge of it, rather than your memories. Let's consider some of the critical aspects of living life with God and experiencing peace in the midst of past suffering.

Begin by Talking to God

One of the most important themes that stands out in the psalms is how the writers of these songs talk to God no matter what is going on and no matter how they feel. The Bible never recommends becoming fatalistic or bottling everything up. Just the opposite. Listen in to these psalms written by David as he struggles with suffering and trauma (the first written as he flees from his own son, who is trying to kill him):

> LORD, how many are my foes!
>   How many rise up against me!
> Many are saying of me,
>   "God will not deliver him." (3 v 1)

> Help, LORD, for no one is faithful anymore;
>   those who are loyal have vanished from the human
>   race.
> Everyone lies to their neighbor;
>   they flatter with their lips
>   but harbor deception in their hearts. (12 v 1-2)

> How long, LORD? Will you forget me forever?
>   How long will you hide your face from me?
> How long must I wrestle with my thoughts
>   and day after day have sorrow in my heart?
>   How long will my enemy triumph over me? (13 v 1-2)

We have looked at just three of 150 psalms! While David does not end his cries and prayers here, he does begin them here—at a place of desperation and hopelessness. Are you able to talk to God in this way? The psalms teach us to seek to make sense of what has happened or is happening within the context of faith in and conversation with God. Their utter honesty shows you that you can talk to God very honestly. If you are going to replace your worries with peace, you must start here. Begin to talk to God.

Acknowledge that Life is Fragile

One thing people who have suffered greatly have is realism about the world they live in. They can move unhelpfully into pessimism and fatalism, but they do not have to. When you live in a war-torn country, you understand how fragile life is. When you go from day to day with one meal at a time, you know how nearby death is. When you have experienced some form of suffering in your past, you understand that this world is not right—that there is something fundamentally flawed about human existence and there are no guarantees that things will go well for you. This is an aspect of wisdom. Wisdom is often associated with old age. Why? Older people have lived longer and they have seen the good, the bad and the ugly of life—they have experienced both the blessings and sufferings that befall everyone sooner or later. Peter was an older man when he wrote these words, quoting the prophet Isaiah:

> All people are like grass,
>   and all their glory is like the flowers of the field;
> the grass withers and the flowers fall, but the word of the
> Lord endures forever.   (1 Peter 1 v 24-25)

Peter knew that life was short. This did not lead to pessimism but realism and vibrant faith in the God who is eternal. If you have suffered deeply, you are onto something that most people aren't. You know that this life is flawed. Strangely, that is a good thing! Now allow that to move you toward God, to renew your faith in him and your need of him.

Remember

The people of Israel were well acquainted with suffering. They experienced the evil of slavery and watched loved ones killed before their very eyes. The period of time that the Old Testament describes was much less than idyllic. Still, in the midst of the heartache, captivities, slavery, injustice and evil, God gave them something to remember. He reminded them again and again of his mercy and kindness, and encouraged them to remember it as well. The prophets would often remind God's people of his saving mercies in the very depths of their sorrow.

Psalm 136 does this by recounting the major redemptive events in Israel's history. This psalm would have been incorporated into the worship of God's people as a means to help them cultivate more powerful images and memories than the suffering they had endured. Psalm 136 begins with creation and moves all the way through the major redemptive moments in Israel's history. After each statement, the people cry: "His love endures forever." This is repeated 26 times over 26 verses.

This is not merely unimaginative repetition! It's worth reading the psalm through. It is a model of how the Christian is to ponder daily all the great things that God has accomplished in our behalf—despite the trauma, sometimes even in and through the trauma; and to reflect on the greatest thing that God has done for us, through the trauma of the cross.

This is what Paul encourages believers to do on a regular basis as they share the Lord's Supper together:

> For I received from the Lord what I also passed on to you: The Lord Jesus, on the night he was betrayed, took bread, and when he had given thanks, he broke it and said, "This is my body, which is for you; do this in remembrance of me." In the same way, after supper he took the cup, saying, "This cup is the new covenant in my blood; do this, whenever you drink it, in

> remembrance of me." For whenever you eat this bread
> and drink this cup, you proclaim the Lord's death until
> he comes. (1 Corinthians 11 v 23-26)

Do you see what is happening? As Christians, we have a grand story that makes sense of and gives hope to our individual stories which are fraught with heartache and sorrow. In our past lies the Lord's death; in our future lies the Lord's coming. We need to tell ourselves this story often enough that the narrative of our life becomes not what has happened to us in those painful past events, but what God has done and is doing and will do for us. We need to enjoy this story often enough that our identity is more shaped by who we are to God than who we were in our past. By celebrating and remembering this as a habit, the old memories, while they may likely never go away, will dissipate into the background and be displaced as the only or main narrative that drives your life.

Fighting the Urge to Forget

Why do we have to practice remembering? Because it is easy to remember the bad, and much more difficult to remember the good. So notice how many times Peter talks in these verses about needing to remember or be reminded of God's grace:

> So I will always remind you of these things, even though
> you know them and are firmly established in the truth
> you now have. I think it is right to refresh your memory
> as long as I live in the tent of this body, because I know
> that I will soon put it aside, as our Lord Jesus Christ has
> made clear to me. And I will make every effort to see that
> after my departure you will always be able to remember
> these things. (2 Peter 1 v 12-15)

Peter was very familiar with the tendency to forget. Therefore, he made every effort to keep the work of Christ before his people. If you are facing past suffering, your tendency will be to forget God's love and grace for you: to forget that he is sovereign, or that he is good. You can't afford to do that. You must ask God to empower you, especially in your weakest moments, to help you to remember.

Live in Community

So far, you may be thinking that this is all good advice, but how do you find the strength to move forward when you constantly feel that you are stuck? This is where God has provided a second relational context for you to grow. The first is with him; the second is with other believers who know you well and love you with great wisdom. It is within the context of the body of Christ that we find the encouragement, prayers and strength to keep moving forward (Hebrews 3 v 12-13; 10 v 24-25). As a church community, we experience fellowship with God and with other believers in Jesus simultaneously. You must have both:

> Let the peace of Christ rule in your hearts, since as members of one body you were called to peace. And be thankful. Let the message of Christ dwell among you richly as you teach and admonish one another with all wisdom through psalms, hymns, and songs from the Spirit, singing to God with gratitude in your hearts.
>
> (Colossians 3 v 15-16)

This is a great picture of the body of Christ working in such a way that each believer is helping other believers to remember and to grow. As the message of grace dwells deeply in our hearts, we encourage each other, and we become more grateful to God and more useful to one another.

As you continue to fight against anxiety that is complicated by past suffering, you may find that a wise counselor with skill and life experience is an additional resource within the broader body of Christ to provide guidance and help. You may want to talk to your pastor or a Christian you respect for advice about which counselor to choose. In addition, you may find that the intensity and depth of your struggle will be helped by medication that can ease the physiological aspects of your anxiety. If so, don't feel ashamed about this. Find wise professional helpers who will work in tandem with those who care for you at your local church.

This is Real

You may be thinking that this sounds all fine and good, but it is not for you, it could not work for you—that you are stuck with your anxiety because you don't think you can move past what has happened to you. I want to encourage you to see that this is easy to think, but is not true. I began this chapter talking about imagined people whose stories were based on those I have met or heard of. I want to finish it by telling you about some real friends of mine.

One was abducted by strangers and taken on a "joy–ride" for hours. She had no idea if she would be raped or killed. To this day, she struggles with anxiety and depression. Another was sexually abused by a family member when he was a teenager. Another was slandered by fellow Christians and shunned by those who knew her. She never had the chance to defend herself or tell her story. It ended her career and she suffered significantly.

What do all of these friends have in common? First, they all still struggle; their memories of past abuse or suffering have not gone away. But second, they have all played a part in this chapter being written. They have taught me what it looks like to face anxiety in the light of past suffering and trauma. This chapter is not armchair theology that has yet to be tested. This chapter is simply a recounting of what has helped people I know and admire. They have not let their past trauma define them, nor the anxiety it produces dominate them. Instead, they have sought, struggled and battled to remember who God is, what he has done for them, and what he will do for them; and they have let themselves be helped by other Christians. They seek to walk faithfully with God the best they can as they depend upon God's grace to carry them on a daily basis. And they tell us that it is possible to have a past that is full of pain, and yet to know peace with Christ.

Questions for Reflection

1. Are there significant events in your past that make your struggle with anxiety more difficult?

2. Are you aware of what "triggers" tend to remind you of these past events? When something triggers a past event, what are your typical responses, and how do they affect your relationships with others and with God?

3. What in this chapter was most helpful?

4. In the section "Transforming Memories," take each sub-section and personalize it to match your own unique experience of worry.

5. Do you need to seek help from others—either in prayer, or in counseling? How will you do so?

5. Worry and your Future

You may have finished the last chapter and said to yourself: "Okay, I get that I don't need to be burdened by my past. But it's not really the past I am worried about; *it is the future*. I don't lie awake at night or struggle to get out of bed in the morning because of yesterday. I can't sleep or get up in the morning because I worry about what is coming today, this week, next week or next year."

We worry about the future because it is uncertain. Worry finds fertile ground to grow in sentences beginning: *What if...?* or: *It might be that...* And life is full of those. Many of us play out whole hypothetical situations about our future, locate the worst-case scenario, and then worry about what hasn't yet happened. Uncertainty is the breeding ground for the roots of anxiety to take hold in your life.

Jesus knows this. That is why his words in Luke 12 v 4-10 are so very important. They actually come just before the commands and encouragements on worry that we looked at from the Gospel of Matthew in chapters 1 and 2. In these verses, Jesus is actually giving you something to worry about! Something about your potential future should startle you and cause deep anxiety within you.

> I tell you, my friends, do not be afraid of those who
> kill the body and after that can do no more. But I will

show you whom you should fear: Fear him who, after
your body has been killed, has authority to throw you
into hell. Yes, I tell you, fear him. Are not five sparrows
sold for two pennies? Yet not one of them is forgotten
by God. Indeed, the very hairs of your head are all
numbered. Don't be afraid; you are worth more than
many sparrows.

I tell you, whoever publicly acknowledges me before
others, the Son of Man will also acknowledge before the
angels of God. But whoever disowns me before others
will be disowned before the angels of God. And everyone
who speaks a word against the Son of Man will be
forgiven, but anyone who blasphemes against the Holy
Spirit will not be forgiven.   (Luke 12 v 4-10)

Something Worth Worrying About

If you think you have problems in the past, they don't even
compare with your potential future problem of being eternally
separated from God. Jesus says that the reality of judgment
and hell is truly something to worry about. If you are going to
"fear" anything or anyone, it should be him who can determine
your eternal destiny: "Fear him who ... has authority to throw
you into hell" (v 5).

This kind of teaching raises all kinds of questions for many
of us. The idea that a loving God would send people to a state of
utter torment is hard to fathom. Whatever happened to peace,
love and understanding? What could Jesus hope to accomplish
by saying these kinds of things to people? The answer is simple
and rather basic. Jesus taught that every human being has an
eternal destination, and will spend eternity in one of two places.
One destination, which he stresses in these verses, is what the

Scriptures refer to as hell. These are sobering words; Jesus says that there is one legitimate thing about which every human being should be deeply worried and anxious. And he says this because he loves you.

Despite the evidence of decay within ourselves, and death all around us, human beings are good at denying their own finitude and the reality of death. And we are even better at denying or suppressing the reality that we live in a moral universe made by a perfect, personal God before whom we must all give an account for our lives. Hebrews 9 v 27 puts this truth in very simple terms when it says: "People are destined to die once, and after that to face judgment." But this is not the way many people think today. Most people either assume that they will avoid judgment or they have completely erased this belief from their minds as a relic of an antiquated, culturally-bound idea that is superstitious, guilt-producing and false.

Yet according to the Bible, the person who spoke most frequently about hell was the most loving person who ever walked the earth—Jesus (look at, for instance, Luke 13 v 22-28; Matthew 13 v 47-50; Matthew 25 v 30, 46). I want to focus here on just one of the times when Jesus spoke clearly of the reality of hell, as he told the story about a rich man and a poor man named Lazarus. The rich man enjoys a life of comfort in the present and avoids caring for the beggar, Lazarus. In the end, the rich man gets what he has lived for his whole life. His life ends and he finds himself in a miserable place of self-centeredness:

> The time came when the beggar died and the angels carried him to Abraham's side. The rich man also died and was buried. In Hades, where he was in torment, he looked up and saw Abraham far away, with Lazarus by his side. So he called to him, "Father Abraham, have pity on

me and send Lazarus to dip the tip of his finger in water and cool my tongue, because I am in agony in this fire."

But Abraham replied, "Son, remember that in your lifetime you received your good things, while Lazarus received bad things, but now he is comforted here and you are in agony. And besides all this, between us and you a great chasm has been set in place, so that those who want to go from here to you cannot, nor can anyone cross over from there to us."

He answered, "Then I beg you, father, send Lazarus to my family, for I have five brothers. Let him warn them, so that they will not also come to this place of torment."

Abraham replied, "They have Moses and the Prophets; let them listen to them."

"No, father Abraham," he said, "but if someone from the dead goes to them, they will repent."

He said to him, "If they do not listen to Moses and the Prophets, they will not be convinced even if someone rises from the dead." (Luke 16 v 22-31)

Jesus says there is a real place, beyond death, of utter separation from God; and he says that it is horrific, and it is irreversible. It is hell. The word "hell" literally referred to a dump outside of Jerusalem where dead bodies and trash were burned all day and night. In Hebrew, this location was called "Gehenna."

The Rightness of Hell

It is good that Jesus tells us about hell so clearly. Without the Bible's honesty, we could easily assume that all is fine and that, when it comes to eternity, there is nothing for us to worry about. Jesus loves you too much to allow you to live in ignorance. He wants you to avoid hell more than he wants you to feel relaxed.

Why does Jesus insist upon teaching about hell? First, the reality of hell reminds us that God is committed to addressing all of the wrongs and injustices that have occurred throughout human history. There is a final day of accounting. No evil deed will escape his judgment. God will exact his judgment in a way that will be completely consistent with his character. He is loving and just, compassionate and perfect.

Another reason is in keeping with the nature of hell itself. Have you ever considered that hell as a final destination is self-chosen? It is a place without God's love, given to those who chose to live without God's love. The reality of hell is actually revealing the end trajectory of the life of a person who is bent on living for themselves. In his book *The Reason for God*, Tim Keller says this:

> "A common image of hell in the Bible is that of fire. Fire
> disintegrates. Even in this life we can see the kind of soul
> disintegration that self-centeredness creates. We know how
> selfishness and self-absorption leads to piercing bitterness,
> nauseating envy, paralyzing anxiety, paranoid thoughts,
> and the mental denials and distortions that accompany
> them. Now ask the question: 'What if when we die we
> don't end, but spiritually our life extends on into eternity?'
> Hell, then, is the trajectory of a soul, living a self-absorbed,
> self-centered life, going on and on forever."

Keller goes on to show how the parable of the rich man and Lazarus bears out this view of hell:

> "Lazarus is a poor man who begs at the gate of a cruel rich
> man. They both die and Lazarus goes to heaven while the

> rich man goes to hell. There he looks up and sees Lazarus
> in heaven 'in Abraham's bosom...'

> "What is astonishing is that though their statuses have now
> been reversed, the rich man seems to be blind to what has
> happened. He still expects Lazarus to be his servant and
> treats him as his water boy."

What is the point of all of Jesus' teaching about hell? He wants to give you something to be worried about! There will be a day of accounting when we will stand before the God of the universe. The reality of hell is not an antiquated doctrine of early, pre-modern Christianity; it is a reality and it should be of deep concern to you. It should keep you up at night. Your ultimate future destiny could possibly be hell. It does not have to be; but it could be.

The Good News about Hell

Is there any good news in the midst of Jesus' teaching about hell? Absolutely! At the very same time that Jesus is actually giving you something to worry about, he is providing a solution to that worry. In the very same context that Jesus is teaching about hell, he gives the good news of God's redeeming grace. He does not want you to end up like the rich man! He reminds his listeners that God does care and that, even more than he loves the sparrow, God loves his people. He has intimate knowledge of you that goes to the very numbering of the hairs on your head! Finally, he reminds you that forgiveness of sins is only a breath away. Luke 12 v 8 is critical:

> I tell you, whoever publicly acknowledges me before
> others, the Son of Man will also acknowledge before the
> angels of God.

Do you see that? The angels who will throw the ungodly into hell (Matthew 13 v 47-50) are also the angels who will welcome into God's presence those who have acknowledged Jesus to be the ruling, rescuing King of eternity.

Let's return to the words in Hebrews 9 I briefly quoted earlier:

> Just as people are destined to die once, and after that to face judgment, so Christ was sacrificed once to take away the sins of many; and he will appear a second time, not to bear sin, but to bring salvation to those who are waiting for him. (v 27-28)

In other words, Jesus' explicit purpose for coming was to deal with the fearful reality of God's judgment of sin and the awful nature of hell. He tells us what to worry about; then he takes away our need to worry. We can be worry free when it comes to the future realities of death and hell.

A Glorious Future

As you bask in the good news that Jesus has come to free you from the worry of hell, it actually gets better. The writers of Scripture provide a glorious picture of what awaits us in heaven. Jesus' mission was not to erase hell from our futures so much as to give us heaven in our futures. Here is just one passage in Scripture—don't skip over it; read it slowly and pause to enjoy and appreciate it:

> Then I saw "a new heaven and a new earth," for the first heaven and the first earth had passed away, and there was no longer any sea. I saw the Holy City, the new Jerusalem, coming down out of heaven from God, prepared as a bride beautifully dressed for her husband. And I heard a loud voice from the throne saying, "Look!

God's dwelling place is now among the people, and he will dwell with them. They will be his people, and God himself will be with them and be their God. 'He will wipe every tear from their eyes. There will be no more death' or mourning or crying or pain, for the old order of things has passed away."

He who was seated on the throne said, "I am making everything new!" Then he said, "Write this down, for these words are trustworthy and true."

He said to me: "It is done. I am the Alpha and the Omega, the Beginning and the End. To the thirsty I will give water without cost from the spring of the water of life. Those who are victorious will inherit all this, and I will be their God and they will be my children.

(Revelation 21 v 1-7)

The Christian can know that this is the future and that it is *their* future. This is where you are heading, because it is what Christ came in the past to secure for your future.

Future Tense Makes us Tense

How does all of this matter as we live in a scary world where bad things happen and good things are not always guaranteed? Take a moment and consider what you are facing this week. Did you sense a degree of anxiety creep into your heart? Symptoms vary based upon the degree of worry. You may experience a loss of appetite, racing thoughts, sadness, paranoia, temptations to check out or become over-controlling. Depression, also, often finds fertile soil in the midst of worry.

How does a future orientation with a focus on heaven help you deal with your current worries? What can we learn from

Scripture as we seek to respond to our own anxieties? Let's return to Matthew 6 v 25-34, Jesus highlights a key component of worry. Look at the phrases in bold:

Therefore I tell you, do not worry about your life, what **you will** eat or drink; or about your body, what **you will** wear. Is not life more than food, and the body more than clothes? Look at the birds of the air; they do not sow or reap or store away in barns, and yet your heavenly Father feeds them. Are you not much more valuable than they? Can any one of you by worrying add a single hour to your life?

And why do you worry about clothes? See how the flowers of the field grow. They do not labor or spin. Yet I tell you that not even Solomon in all his splendor was dressed like one of these. If that is how God clothes the grass of the field, which is here today and tomorrow is thrown into the fire, will he not much more clothe you—you of little faith? So do not worry, saying, "**What shall we** eat?" or "**What shall we** drink?" or "**What shall we** wear?" For the pagans run after all these things, and your heavenly Father knows that you need them. But seek first his kingdom and his righteousness, and all these things will be given to you as well. Therefore **do not worry about tomorrow,** for tomorrow will worry about itself. Each day has enough trouble of its own.

One of the reasons we worry is because we can't control the future.

Notice the use of the future tense: what you *will* eat, drink or wear. Depending on your context, your worries can be more immediate and focus on physical survival. If you are relatively confident that your basic needs will be met, your worries could spill over into other kinds of needs. *Will people like me? Will I measure up? Will my spouse be faithful? Will our kids turn out okay? Will we have enough money to retire? I wonder how and when I will die.* The questions can come to us on an endless rotation, or there may be one or two that grab us and won't let go.

Remember, though, that the Bible is a future-dominated book. Christianity's view of history is linear, not circular like many other worldviews and belief systems. And the Bible is packed with promises made in history, about the future. From Genesis to Revelation, the Bible is brimming with hope. One of the biggest promises in Scripture is: "I am making everything new" (Revelation 21 v 5). One day, Jesus' people will see him as he returns to this world, and announces: *I **have** made everything new.* It is the great pinnacle of the Christian message.

What are your biggest worries about the future? Jesus wants you to grasp that it is not illness, or your retirement, ability to send your children to college, achieving success in your career or securing respect from your peers. They pale in comparison with what your eternal, ultimate future destination will be. Will it be hell or will it be heaven? What happens to you in your lifetime cannot compare with where you will spend eternity. Jesus is wants to help us see clearly; to appreciate that in him, we have no need to be worried about the grim and terrible reality of hell. Instead, we live with a secure assurance that we will spend the rest of our lives (after physical death) in the very presence of God, the heavenly host and our redeemed brothers and sisters in Christ. And so, Paul says in 2 Corinthians 4 v 16-18:

> We do not lose heart. Though outwardly we are wasting away, yet inwardly we are being renewed day by day. For

our light and momentary troubles are achieving for us
an eternal glory that far outweighs them all. So we fix our
eyes not on what is seen, but on what is unseen, since
what is seen is temporary, but what is unseen is eternal.

People have searched far and wide, but nowhere do you find this kind of hope in any other philosophy or life, self-help book or religious system. The Christian gospel is the only place that offers you this kind of perspective.

Is this *Your* Future?

This may be a good point to ask yourself the questions:

- "Can I be sure this is my future?"
- "Have I acknowledged Jesus as my Redeemer and King, and asked him to forgive me of my failures and best efforts to save myself?"
- "Do I know that the Holy Spirit is in me, empowering me and reminding me that he is a deposit guaranteeing my complete redemption one day when Jesus returns in all of his glory?"

If the answers are "No" or "I'm not sure," this would be a good time to find a Christian who you trust, and start a conversation with them with the aim of coming to terms with who Jesus is, and what your relationship with him will be. These are life-and-death matters, as well as the only way to find comfort and refuge in your present life and current worries.

Think about it like this. If your future between here and the grave is all there is, it would be worth worrying about. If there is an eternity beyond the grave to be spent in hell, separated from the love of God, that should be the only thing we should worry about. Wonderfully, if you're trusting Christ, neither of these futures is yours; so you shouldn't worry about the first (because eternity dwarfs this life) and you don't need to worry about the second (because heaven, not hell, is your destiny). So in the ups and downs of life, the stresses and strains of the uncertain future, let the certainty of your eternal future be what you cling to. Talk to your Father to thank him for these truths, and remind yourself of these truths. You may be concerned about next week and next month and next year. But do not be over-concerned about it. Make sure your focus is on your eternal future, and enjoy the assurance that, whatever life brings you in 20 or 50 years, in 200 years it will bring you eternal glory with Christ. Bathe your soul in these truths and talk to your heavenly Father about them. Thank him for them, and set the future aspects you naturally worry about in their proper perspective.

You have enough on your plate. You also have One who knows what is on your plate and what you need in order to move forward today. That doesn't mean it will be easy, but it does mean you have hope to press into today because you know the end of the story. May God grant you grace to embrace the living truths that, if you belong to Jesus, hell has no power over you, and one day you are going to see him face to face, and enjoy him forever.

Are you beginning to see why Jesus can say: "Do not worry"—and how you can begin to obey him?

Questions for Reflection

1. Most worry is future oriented. What unknown future possibilities do you tend to worry about?

2. Did you find it surprising that Jesus actually encourages you to worry about something? Have you ever really worried about what happens to you when you die?

3. How has the reality of heaven helped you as you thought about your worries?

4. Is there a particular future issue that you need to use the realities of hell and heaven to get into perspective?

5. What one thing in this chapter would you like to talk to God about?

6. Worry and your Present

Your past sins have been taken care of in Christ's death and resurrection—you don't need to worry about your past.

And Christ's death and resurrection have secured a certain and eternal home for you in eternity—you don't need to worry about your future.

These truths should intersect your daily life in the present. And yet they can seem a bit removed from your day-to-day experience. It is one thing to know something. It is quite another to live it. "What about right now?" you ask. "What about the financial, relational or health issues that are on my plate today?"

Perhaps you picked up this book and you have just found that out your teenage son or daughter has decided to live a very different kind of life than you had hoped. Maybe you have just learned that your job is being phased out or you have been fired. Maybe you have just been betrayed by a close friend or family member and you wonder if you will ever be able to trust another person again. Maybe you have a hospital appointment next week for some tests, and it's all you can think about. The potential scenarios are endless. You fill in the blanks. The big question is: *How in the world can I be engaged with these realities, but not be plagued by worry?* We come back to the question at the start of the book: is Jesus' command not to worry achievable, even if it is desirable?

Promises, Promises

Not too long ago, the newest version of the iPhone was released. If you watched the video of the CEO of Apple, Tim Cook, talking about the new device, and watched the attendees gasp with excitement, you would have thought they had found a cure for cancer! The announcement was filled with promises about how the device was going to change people's lives. I was surprised they didn't have an altar call and baptize people!

People want something to look forward to. They want to expect great things. It is what excites us and keeps us going. People need hope right now. It is how God has wired us. Every human being knows, deep down, that they were built for something greater than themselves, and for something greater than this mortal life (Ecclesiastes 3 v 11). We all live with some sense that there must be more. The iPhone unveiling is tapping into that innate human impulse for something more. C. S. Lewis wrote in *Mere Christianity*:

> *"If I find in myself a desire which no experience in this world can satisfy, the most probable explanation is that I was made for another world."*

As we face our present challenges, we find hope in the here and now through the promises of God. God's purposes and plans for you, and your day today, are bigger than you could ever imagine. The challenge is remembering that in the midst of daily life. We can be duped so quickly. And the antidote is to remember God's promises:

> His divine power has given us everything we need for life and godliness through our knowledge of him who called us by his own glory and goodness. Through these he has given us his very great and precious promises, so that through them you may participate in the divine nature

and escape the corruption in the world caused by evil
desires.   (2 Peter 1 v 3-4, NIV84)

Why has God given us his promises? "So that ... you may participate in the divine nature and escape the corruption in the world caused by evil desires." God's promises give us the ability to relate to God, enjoy God, and face our problems without giving in to temptation. When we know what God has promised to be doing in, for and through us, every day, we find our anxieties are replaced by peace.

So what are some of God's promises that you need as you face your present worries? Let's consider a few of the bigger ones.

God Promises... to be at Work in You

Let's start by looking at the most audacious of God's promises to you. What kind of future does God have in store for you?

We are children of God, and what we will be has not
yet been made known. But we know that when Christ
appears, we shall be like him, for we shall see him as he
is. All who have this hope in him purify themselves, just
as he is pure.   (1 John 3 v 2-3)

The entire trajectory of your life is ultimately to be conformed into the likeness of Christ. Nothing can stop this from happening. Because you belong to him, you will one day be like him in character. That means you can read the Gospels and see Christ's love, his passion, his gentleness, his sensitivity, his wisdom, his forgiveness, his courage and his strength; and think... one day, that's what you will be like. What a prospect!

But how is that going to happen? Paul tells us:

> And we know that in all things God works for the good
> of those who love him, who have been called according
> to his purpose. For those God foreknew he also
> predestined to be conformed to the image of his Son,
> that he might be the firstborn among many brothers and
> sisters. (Romans 8 v 28-29)

Do you see how John and Paul talk about the same thing? John tells you that one day you will be like Christ in terms of your character. Paul tells you that God is going to accomplish that ultimate goal in the day-by-day moments of your life. There is nothing that can happen today that God will not use for your good; and by good, Paul means becoming more and more like Jesus. All the good things and blessings, and all the hard things and the losses; in all things God is working for the good of those who love him. Nothing will be able to stop that from happening!

I remember when my daughter was a teenager and I was trying to figure out how to be a parent to a teenage girl. I didn't always get things right, and when things were difficult I was prone to become anxious about how my daughter might be turning out. I would find myself asking: *Am I doing the right thing? Am I being too strict? Am I being too lenient?*

On one occasion, my daughter did not receive my advice very well and stomped out of the room muttering something under her breath. I assumed it was something disrespectful. My usual response would have been to get agitated and try to confront her in the moment. Rarely did that go well. Instead, on this occasion, I found myself functionally applying Romans 8 v 28-29 to my life. Instead of snapping at my daughter, I began to talk to God. I uttered words like these: *Father, I know you love me and my daughter. I know that you use all things to change us and make us more like Christ: the good and the challenging. I know that you are using this moment between me and my daughter to make me more like Jesus. Help me to acknowledge you and your work in this moment. Give me grace to love my daughter. Give me grace to not be over-concerned or anxious about what she may become.*

That simple conversation with God enabled me to remain calm. Later, my daughter and I had a positive conversation about how we were both struggling to navigate the choppy waters of the teenage years. That would not have been the discussion that we would have had in the heat of the moment! Do you see what was happening? By turning a theoretical belief in Romans 8 v 28-29 into a functional reality, I was able to trust God to be at work instead of being anxious that my attempts to parent were not working; I could know he was in control instead of feeling the need to seize control myself. And later, I could look back and see how he had used a difficult situation that I would not have chosen to make me a little more patient, a little more trusting, a little more like Jesus. God promises to be at work in you today, in every situation, to make you more like Jesus.

Take a moment and put these truths into words that you can speak to your Father in heaven: *Father, I know that there are many things to worry about, but I thank you that you are orchestrating all things to be used for my good and to make me like Jesus. Lord, have mercy on me and give me grace to live in light of this promise today.*

God Promises... to be Faithful in Hardship

Here is another promise that God has provided to encourage you right now, no matter what you are facing today:

> No temptation has overtaken you except what is
> common to mankind. And God is faithful; he will not let
> you be tempted beyond what you can bear. But when you
> are tempted, he will also provide a way out so that you
> can endure it. (1 Corinthians 10 v 13)

Notice that Paul is not saying that God will take you out of a
season of trial. If that is what he meant, he would not end the
sentence with "so that you can endure it." What Paul is saying
is that God will be ever-faithful in your season of trial and he
will provide sufficient grace in the present so that you may
live under the weight of the trial and endure it. So you can
walk one day at a time with what you have on your plate. John
Newton described one of the ways that God is faithful in the
following way:

> *"I compare the troubles which we have to undergo in the
> course of the year—to a great bundle of sticks, far too
> large for us to lift. But God does not require us to carry the
> whole bundle at once. He mercifully unties the bundle,
> and gives us first one stick, which we are to carry today;
> and then another, which we are to carry tomorrow, and so
> forth. We can easily manage our troubles, if we would only
> carry the trouble appointed for each day. But the load will
> be too heavy for us—if we carry yesterday's burden over
> again today, and then add the burden of tomorrow to the
> weight, before we are required to bear it."*

God is not going to ask you to do anything today that he knows
you cannot do. He is not going to tempt you to worry in a way
that you cannot resist. This does not mean that it will be easy
or that he will relieve all painful circumstances. It does mean
that he will be faithful to you in the midst of the difficulty.

Take a moment and put these truths into words that you

speak to your Father in heaven: *Father, I know that there are many things to worry about, but I thank you that you promise to not place upon me more than I can bear. While I know that this does not mean that life will always be easy, it does mean that you know my frame, my strengths and weaknesses, and you will not crush me under a weight I cannot withstand. Lord, have mercy on me and give me grace to live in light of this promise today.*

God Promises... to be With You Each Day

Have you ever thought how strange it is that Jesus, the night before he died, as he explained to his closest friends that he would be taken from them in the most brutal way imaginable, said to them:

> Do not let your hearts be troubled ... Do not let your
> hearts be troubled and do not be afraid. (John 14 v 1, 27)

What reasons does he give? First, because he is leaving them to open the way to eternity, and prepare a place for them there. But second, because:

> I will ask the Father, and he will give you another
> advocate to help you and be with you forever—the Spirit
> of truth. The world cannot accept him, because it neither
> sees him nor knows him. But you know him, for he
> lives with you and will be in you. I will not leave you as
> orphans; I will come to you. (v 16-18)

I do not think there is any other world religion that speaks as boldly about the presence of the divine with the believer as the Christian faith. At the heart of Christianity is a relationship. The ethical demands of Christianity are not the foundation of the Christian religion; a relationship with God is. God has promised to be with us.

The classic hymn *How Firm a Foundation* puts it beautifully:

The soul that on Jesus has leaned for repose,
I will not, I will not desert to its foes;
That soul, though all hell should endeavor to shake,
I'll never, no never, no never forsake.

All of this means that while you may feel that you are all alone, you are not. God, in Christ, is with you through the ongoing work of the Spirit. He is not only with you and for you, but *in* you. The use of the word *in* is very important. It is the fulfillment of the entire Bible. Central to God's promises in the Old Testament is this commitment: "I will take you as my own people, and I will be your God" (Exodus 6 v 7). In Christ, this has been fulfilled in a way that the Old Testament believer longed for. If you are a Christian, God is living in you by the Holy Spirit. You can't get much closer than that! So whatever you could be troubled by today, you will not go through it alone. You will have the Spirit for company.

Take a moment and put these truths into words that you speak to your Father in heaven: *Father, I know that there are many things to worry about, but I thank you that you are with me. You have sworn to never leave me or forsake me, and that today's troubles are no match for your daily care for me and presence with me. Lord, have mercy on me and give me grace to live in light of this promise today.*

God Promises… to Love You as His Child

It is one thing to know that you are treated with forgiveness and that God will live within you. That ought to be enough. But God's promises are even better. He promises to embrace you as his own and treat you with the same fatherly love that he gives his own dear Son, Jesus. Listen as Jesus prays to his and your heavenly Father for you.

> My prayer is not for them alone. I pray also for those who will believe in me through their message, that all of them may be one, Father, just as you are in me and I am in you. May they also be in us so that the world may believe that you have sent me. I have given them the glory that you gave me, that they may be one as we are one—I in them and you in me—so that they may be brought to complete unity. Then the world will know that you sent me and have loved them even as you have loved me.   (John 17 v 20-23)

Did you catch that last phrase? Read the last six words again. Jesus says that his Father in heaven loves you with the same love with which he loves his own dear Son. And it is utterly shocking that God calls us his children. It would have sounded offensive to a first-century Jew; it would have seemed too intimate for a believer to describe his relationship with the holy, perfect God in this way. Yet, the New Testament uses this "father/child" metaphor as one of the most prominent ways to describe every Christian's relationship with God:

> See what great love the Father has lavished upon us, that we should be called children of God! And that is what we are!   (1 John 3 v 1; see also John 1 v 12-13;
> Romans 8 v 15-17; Galatians 3 v 26)

Are you anxious? God loves you right now with the same affection he has for his own Son. While that may not sink in and change you immediately, a life that is lived with this truth abiding more and more at its foundation will be a life that is on a very different trajectory than one that does not know this. Scripture is replete with promises of God's embrace.

Take a moment and put these truths into words that you can speak to your Father in heaven: *Father, I know that there are many things to worry about today, but I thank you that you embrace me as your child and shower the same love on me that you do on Jesus. You have adopted me as your child and made Jesus my elder brother. Lord, have mercy on me and give me grace to live in light of this promise today.*

God Promises... to Provide all You Need

One of the most challenging things that you will struggle with as you fight your worries is a confidence that you have all of the resources you need on a daily basis. If having what you need depends on you to provide it, of course you will worry; and if and when you realize that you cannot provide what you or a loved one needs (whether materially, or emotionally), you will worry all the more. But God promises to give you all you need, each day, between here and heaven:

> He who did not spare his own Son, but gave him up for us all—how will he not also, along with him, graciously give us all things? (Romans 8 v 32)

This is not saying that God will give you everything you want, or think you need. God knows what you truly need: what it is that you require today to live life with faith in his Son, still on the pathway to home and to heaven. He will provide all you need; anything you do not have, you did not in truth need. He will give you the courage, the wisdom, the love and the endurance to keep walking in faith. You can look at your day, or your week, and as you identify the potential worries, you can say to yourself: *God will graciously give me all I need, whatever that may be.*

And it is important to add: *God will graciously give others who love him what they need, too.* He is not relying on you to do that! He will do what is best for your family and for your church, and he will do that regardless of whether you lie awake worrying about your responsibilities, or crush yourself trying to do everything for everyone.

Take a moment and put these truths into words that you can speak to your Father in heaven: *Father, I know that there are many things I could worry about today, but I thank you that you have promised to provide for my every need. Thank you that your provision does not depend on my performance, but on your grace. Thank you most of all that you have given me yourself. Lord, have mercy on me and give me grace to live in light of this promise right now.*

Whistling in the Dark?

But... are these promises anything more than whistling in the dark? When people feel alone or scared, they make some happy-sounding noise to make themselves feel better, to change the mood, to make it seem that they are not on their own. God's promises are wonderful truths to sing out loud, not just to yourself, but to the One who made them in the first place. But are they real?

This is the sheer beauty of the life of faith. It is not something that is just in your own head, nor merely another form of positive thinking that you do all by yourself or with the help of a support group. It is a conversation with the real, personal, promise-making and promise-keeping Redeemer God.

See how Paul states this emphatically in Romans 8 v 32:

> He who did not spare his own Son, but gave him up for us all—how will he not also, along with him, graciously give us all things?

How can you know that God will give you all you need, that you're not just whistling in the dark? How can you be sure God is really keeping his promises to be with you, and be at work in you, and not test you beyond what you can bear? Because he has already given you his most precious gift. He has already done what was most costly to himself. He has already given you his Son.

Do you see Paul's argument? He is arguing from greater to lesser. If God would give his Son to die on the cross for your sins, do you really think that he would now withhold other critical but lesser things to strengthen you in your moment of need?

Human promises tend to fail. For all the fervor of the launch, Apple's iPhone quickly ran into problems with its operating system. It did change its owners' lives; but only by preventing them from making calls on their cellphone! We have learned in our age to be fairly cynical whenever we are offered something that sounds too good to be true.

Just because you make a promise does not mean that it is grounded in reality. And that is why the Bible constantly points us to the cross and the empty tomb as the reality in which all God's promises are grounded. We look to those past events to give us great certainty that God will keep his promises to us in the present. As Paul puts it:

> No matter how many promises God has made, they are
> "Yes" in Christ. (2 Corinthians 1 v 20)

It is imperative that we grasp these promises because if we don't, we will live poverty-stricken lives, spiritually. J. C. Ryle was an English bishop who uttered this warning in his book *Holiness*:

> *"A child may be born heir to a great fortune and yet never be aware of his riches; may live childish, die childish, and*

> *never know the greatness of his possessions. And so also*
> *a man may be a babe in Christ's family, think as a babe,*
> *speak as a babe, and, though saved, never enjoy a lively*
> *hope, or know the real privileges of his inheritance."*

If what Ryle says is true, then you must spend some time looking at these great and precious promises that remind you of your inheritance, privileges and spiritual wealth in Christ, and then spend time looking at the cross to remind yourself that these promises are not merely wonderful, they are true. They are made by the God who is utterly trustworthy. And because they are true, there is no need to worry in the present, because this God has your back.

How to Enjoy Peace

So how do we put these promises to work in our lives right now? God does not want you to be worried about anything today. Listen to how Paul encourages us to put these things into practice:

> Rejoice in the Lord always. I will say it again: Rejoice! Let your gentleness be evident to all. The Lord is near. Do not be anxious about anything, but in every situation, by prayer and petition, with thanksgiving, present your requests to God. And the peace of God, which transcends all understanding, will guard your hearts and minds in Christ Jesus. (Philippians 4 v 4-7)

Paul's exhortation was not written in an ivory tower. It was written in a prison cell! He was not in a good place, himself. Yet he is exhorting you to rejoice, be thankful, not be anxious and pray—and to know peace as you do so. The reason he could do this was because Paul knew who God was and is. His encouragement is grounded in the true promises of God, which will prompt great thanksgiving and lead to dependent prayer.

Prayer is no easy practice, especially when you are feeling anxious. But Paul commands you to pray instead of worry. It is the exact thing he is fighting to do from a jail cell in Philippi. While it will not be easy or happen automatically, it will emerge as you ground your heart in your relationship with God, and start to express an active faith in the moments of your daily life. Be encouraged as you look at Paul and all of the reasons you have to combat your worry.

And then you will find yourself experiencing what Paul sets out here: not just less worry, but more joy and more peace. The Christian life never calls you to a negative without giving you positive, more compelling things to hope in. Even though your circumstances may not change (Paul remained in prison), your perspective, heart orientation and emotions will, as you allow anxiety to give way to celebrating God's grace. In a sense, the goal is not to worry less, but to rejoice more. The power of the truth and hope of God's goodness and presence will begin to dispel and destroy the power of your anxiety.

Paul knew "the Lord is near." He allowed that promise of God to shape his emotions, rather than being directed by his circumstances. God's promises cut our over-concerns down to size. They bring us to prayer. And they provide us with joy-filled peace.

Why Worry?

We all have a past, we all face a future, and we all live in a present. Each provides us with reasons to worry. And yet the gospel removes all those reasons. Your past is forgiven, and will continue to be. Your future is secure, in eternity. The God who sent his Son to die for you has promised to be with you, changing you, providing for you, protecting you and loving you today, in your present.

You might say that, in truth, there is absolutely nothing for you to worry about!

Questions for Reflection

1. The three chapters before this one, about worry and your past and future, are intended to help you in the present. What two or three things from those chapters have been most helpful?

2. This chapter is even more focused on your present struggles. Which promises did you find most helpful for you in your own particular circumstances?

3. The illustration about me and my daughter was very practical and connected to simple things in the course of a normal day. Where can you begin to see God prompting you to connect one or more of his promises to an aspect of your ordinary life that tends to cause anxiety?

4. Ask several friends to share with you two or three promises that help them face their worries. Add them to your list.

5. How might you be an encouragement to someone else who is struggling with worry (whether they realize it or not)?

7. How to Begin to Change

Grace-laden Thanksgiving

"Grace makes beauty out of ugly things," sings Bono in U2's song "Grace." In an interview quoted in the book *Bono on Bono: Conversations with Michka Assayas*, he added: "I'd be in big trouble if Karma [the idea that good intentions and deeds contribute to future happiness, while bad ones contribute to future suffering] was going to finally be my judge. It doesn't excuse my mistakes, but I'm holding out for Grace."

If you are united to Christ by faith, you live with great future hope and also present gratitude because God is at work in you, even if it is not easily apparent to you. Sometimes it is hard to see the gold because of the remaining dross. But grace— God's undeserved, overwhelming, unstoppable kindness—is at work, making you more and more beautiful.

If you have read this far, I want to be very personal. As you look at your life and see your track record, no doubt, if you are like me, you will have plenty to be ashamed of. You and I have done things we regret. We have committed sins we wished we had never committed, and we struggle every day to fight a host of temptations. And, yes, we have ignored Jesus' command not to worry, because we've over-loved created things and lived as though there were not a God who is in control and who is always acting in love. Yet, in all of that, God is working in you and changing you. Take a moment and give thanks for God's ever-present grace in your life. This grace is rooted in the forgiveness of your sins through Jesus and his enabling strength in you by the Holy Spirit. If you belong to Jesus, you are not the same person you would have been without him. This is vitally important to keep in mind as you face down your worries. As a way of encouraging his readers, Paul says this in Philippians 1 v 3-6:

> I thank my God every time I remember you. In all my prayers for all of you, I always pray with joy because of your partnership in the gospel from the first day until now, being confident of this, that he who began a good work in you will carry it on to completion until the day of Christ Jesus.

In this chapter, I'm going to ask you to spend time in prayerful self-examination. That can be difficult, humbling, even painful. But before we begin, spend some time in prayerful thanksgiving for the good work that God is doing in your life. Yes, you still have much to learn and more growing to go through, but don't let that truth trump the equal truth that God is graciously changing you, and will never leave or forsake you along the way. You will be carried by him as he enables you to strive to grow in grace. There is no excuse for not changing, because God is at work; but equally, there is nothing to stop you from changing, because God is at work.

Grace-laden Self-examination

With God's present work in us clearly in view, let us move forward and engage in grace-laden self-examination. The Bible calls us not only to consider what we do, but our motives for what we do. It is, of course, possible to do the "right thing" with sinful motives. So Paul says:

> Do nothing out of selfish ambition or vain conceit, but
> in humility consider others better than yourselves ...
> Your attitude should be the same as that of Christ Jesus.
>
> (Philippians 2 v 3, 5, NIV84)

Paul is clearly calling each of us to engage in careful self-examination to see if we are living consistently in line with the grace that we have been given in Christ. We need to "work out [our] salvation with fear and trembling" (v 12). While our salvation is completely free, it was not cheap. It cost Jesus his very life. We are not to treat that cheaply just because it is free. Being a Christian means we will be motivated to change—not only in what we do, but in how we think and feel, and most foundationally in our hearts and what we live for.

Roots and Fruit

Let's begin our thinking about self-examination by looking at Jesus' words in Luke 6 v 43-45:

> No good tree bears bad fruit, nor does a bad tree bear
> good fruit. Each tree is recognized by its own fruit.
> People do not pick figs from thornbushes, or grapes
> from briers. A good man brings good things out of the
> good stored up in his heart, and the evil man brings
> evil things out of the evil stored up in his heart. For the
> mouth speaks what the heart is full of.

Do you see what Jesus is saying? Jesus uses the word picture of a tree and its roots which produce a certain kind of fruit. He then draws a connection between trees and people. Human beings are driven by what is going on in their hearts. Their hearts are like the roots of a tree. Whatever root system is in place will determine what kind of fruit will grow. In the same way, the condition of the heart of a human being will drive their response to their circumstances; this includes their behavior, thoughts, emotions, words and body language.

It is important to define what the Bible means when it uses the word "heart." The word heart in the Bible typically refers to the very core of who a person is. Other words like "mind," "will," "soul" and "strength" are talking about the same part of a person. It is their spiritual core. The condition of the heart is connected to what you believe, daydream about, adore, or live for (the Bible calls this "worship"). Whatever this is will determine your behavior.

So in order to know what you are living for, you must examine your words, emotions and behavior, and work backwards to determine what is motivating you. Jesus says that you can see what a person lives for, loves, and adores based upon what comes out of their mouths. A person's speech or behavior is an expression of the condition of their soul no less than the apples on a tree are the supreme indicator of the type of tree it is.

The Heart of the Issue

What does this have to do with worry? Everything. The Bible says that if you are a wise person, you will make the effort to connect your behavior to your core commitments or beliefs. Proverbs 20 v 5 says:

> The purposes of a person's heart are deep waters, but
> one who has insight draws them out.

When you do this, it is the start of the change process. Until you are able to draw a line from your behavior and what is driving it, you can't call out to God for grace to enable you to turn away from what you are living for and find the grace of Christ you need to start changing.

It is no accident that just before Jesus' teaching on worry in the Gospel of Matthew he talks about storing up treasure in heaven (Matthew 6 v 19-24). And Luke places the parable of the rich fool who stored up treasures on earth but was "not rich toward God," just before his account of Jesus' teaching about worry (Luke 12 v 13-21). What you worry about is a good indicator to what you truly value and rely upon.

When you find that you are filled with anxiety, there is something going on in your heart. You are finding value in something other than Christ; and because you think it might be taken away, you are filled with anxiety. Or you are putting your trust somewhere other than in Christ (yourself, or someone else, or "chance") and because you cannot truly trust it, you are feeling worried. Let's read Matthew 6 v 19-24 and start to see how worry can reveal what you are living for. This will provide a window into how you need to grow and change if you are going to face your anxiety with growing humility, strength and confidence.

> Do not store up for yourselves treasures on earth, where moths and vermin destroy, and where thieves break in and steal. But store up for yourselves treasures in heaven, where moths and vermin do not destroy, and where thieves do not break in and steal. For where your treasure is, there your heart will be also.

> The eye is the lamp of the body. If your eyes are healthy, your whole body will be full of light. But if your eyes are unhealthy, your whole body will be full of darkness. If then the light within you is darkness, how great is that darkness!

> No one can serve two masters. Either you will hate the one and love the other, or you will be devoted to the

one and despise the other. You cannot serve both God and money.

Do you see what Jesus is saying? Just before he talks about worry, he talks about what you treasure. If you treasure something that is not stable and lasting, you will naturally be anxious because it may be taken away from you. On the other hand, if you treasure something that is permanent and unchanging, you will not be anxious because it can't be taken from you; nor will it decay or disappear.

Let's get practical and personal. What do you worry about? Have you ever taken the time to draw lines between your worry and what you are living for? If not, this is exactly what God wants you to do. As you do this, you will appreciate more God's grace and his stability in the face of the unstable things in which we tend to place our confidence. It will increase how much you value God's unchanging, stable and consistent love for you in Christ.

A Simple Word of Caution

Before you look at your own anxieties, let me tell you about a friend of mine who is afraid to fly in airplanes. He went years avoiding flying. Why is he so anxious about it? If you are not careful, you may run straight to the obvious answer: that he is afraid to fly because he is afraid to die. You might consider encouraging him that because of Jesus' resurrection, death is not the end and therefore he should not be afraid. While true, this answer for my friend was simplistic, unhelpful and off-putting. In fact, his anxiety about flying is not driven by his fear of death. He is a Christian and he is convinced that death is not the final reality. While he does not want to die, he is not gripped by anxiety over the prospect of his ultimate death.

So why is he afraid to fly? After some time, self-examination and help from a caring counselor, he located the root of his anxiety. His anxiety was not driven by a fear of death, but by how foolishly he thought he would act as the plane plummeted to earth! He could not bear to think about what others would think of him as he "freaked out" during the plane's descent and ultimate crash.

In other words, his anxiety was driven by how others would view him. He began to see that this was true in other areas of his life. What he lived for and worshiped was his own good reputation and how others viewed him! And so he needed to believe in his heart that his value was rooted in being a child of God, and that God's opinion of him was the only one that ultimately and eternally mattered.

Not surprisingly, once he saw this and began to repent and grow in grace, change started to happen. He flies now. That does not mean that he does not struggle with anxiety whenever he gets on a plane. But he does so very differently. He is watchful of his own struggles and prayerful at the same time. Before, God was not even on the radar. Now, he is learning to take his anxieties to God.

As you look over your life, be careful not to draw quick conclusions about what you live for when it comes to your worries. The following examples are basic. Don't let their simplicity tempt you to draw simplistic conclusions about what your worries say about what you live for.

Working Out your Worries

Let's take a few common areas of worry, and add into the mix the discussion in chapters 3 – 6 on past, present and future worries. The specific categories are all areas where we may have experienced some degree of suffering (and we'll think more about suffering in the next chapter). These questions are not to minimize the suffering, but to see how your suffering has opened you up to temptation and struggle with worry.

Worry and Finances

Let's start with something common to us all. Do you ever worry about finances? What are the signs of worry about finances? Do you lie awake worrying about your income and expenses? Do you fret over bills? Does your personal well-being and emotional state rise and fall with the state of your bank balance or the stock market? If so, this could be an indication that money, financial security and social status are the things that you really live for, more than the living God.

- **Past:** Are you worried because your last capital investment went belly up, or because you grew up in a family where money was always very tight, or was considered the only indicator of true success and security?
- **Present:** Are you worried because you just received a bill that you did not budget for?
- **Future:** Are you worried about whether you will have enough to pay for your children's college or your retirement?

Take some time to think about your typical response to your finances. What does that say about what you can be tempted to live for more than the living God? How does the truth about what God has done for your past, is doing in your present and will do in your future provide you with help as you face your worries?

Worry and Relationships

Do you find yourself worrying whether you will be liked by others? Do you worry about what others think of you? Do you find yourself highly critical of others? Perhaps you find yourself deeply fearful, wondering if others like you. Perhaps you sabotage your relationships and reject others before they can potentially reject you. Do you tend to smother other people because you are overly needy for their approval? Do you place expectations on others that are unrealistic and find that you are angry, or friendless and lonely?

- **Past:** Are you worried because your last friendship, relationship, marriage ended poorly? Maybe you have experienced deep rejection or even abusive treatment.
- **Present:** Are you worried because you don't know if you have the ability to love your spouse or navigate a current conflict at work, or be the friend someone needs you to be?
- **Future:** Are you worried because you wonder if you will ever find a spouse? Do you worry that a friendship you currently have will eventually go downhill? Are you worried that you may lose someone close to you?

Take some time to think about your typical responses to relationships in your life. What does that say about what you are easily tempted to live for, other than God?

Worry and Children

If you have children, what kind of parent are you? Are you hyper-vigilant and anxious about your children and their behavior? Do you find yourself over-compensating to fill in gaps that were left open in your own childhood?

- **Past:** Are you worried that you will make the same mistakes your parents made? Are you worried that you have already made so many mistakes and hurt your children?
- **Present:** Are you worried about an issue your child is going through? Are you noticing some behaviors that are not looking so good? Are you wrestling with a decision you must make on their behalf?
- **Future:** Are you worried because you can't protect your children from the inevitable hurts, sufferings and losses that they will experience in their lives? Are you worried about who they might marry or if they will ever get married?

Take some time to think about your style of parenting. What does that say about what you are living for?

Worry and Marriage

What kind of spouse are you? Are you needy and demanding? Are you anxious about the way your spouse treats and responds to you? Do you have unrealistic expectations of your spouse that place undue burdens on them that they were never able nor intended to provide? Is the temperature of your relationship always on the brink of boiling over?

- **Past:** Are you worried because of mistakes you made in past relationships or in your current marriage?
- **Present:** Are you worried because you can't seem to face the conflict that is happening in your marriage right now, or because of something your spouse is going through that you cannot help with?
- **Future:** Are you worried because you wonder if your marriage can survive for the long-haul, or

about what you may have to face as a couple as you
grow older?

Take some time to think about your responses to difficulties
in your marriage (either real or hypothetical future ones).
What does that say about what you are living for?

Worry and Control

Where do you find yourself struggling with being out of
control? Do you "check out" or become over-controlling? In
what ways do you "check out" or become hyper-vigilant?

- **Past:** Are you worried because you experienced
  being out of control in your past because someone
  took advantage of you or you failed miserably at
  something you tried?
- **Present:** Are you worried because you can't see a way
  out of a situation that you have no power to change?
- **Future:** Are you worried because you always predict
  the worst possible scenario for most situations?

Take some time to think about your attitude towards control,
and toward being "out of control." What does that say about
what you are living for?

A Window into your Soul

Remind yourself of chapter 2 and pages 23-24 and Jesus' teaching
about the kingdom of God (it might be worth re-reading those
pages). Remember he said you can't love two masters at the
same time? Jesus is teaching us to live life in light of his return
as King to establish his kingdom. His kingdom is at odds with
the kingdoms of the world, and his kingdom is one in which
worry has no place. Since the kingdom of God has come initially

in Jesus, change is possible. But the kingdom of God will not be completely ushered in until Jesus returns again.

That means we live in an "in between" time. Theologians call this the "already and not yet." The kingdom of God has already come in Jesus' first coming but it has not yet been fully realized nor will it be until he comes for a second time. In this "in between" time, the question that we must ask ourselves is: *Which kingdom has the greatest influence over us; the kingdom of God, or the kingdom of this world?* Jesus shows that worry is a way for you to assess the state of your own soul as it relates to that question. By looking at what you worry about, you can become a person of understanding who tackles the deep matters of your own heart by the grace of Christ at work in you by his Spirit. Worry can be a window into your soul, revealing what you are functionally living for.

So let this chapter lead you in two ways. First, let it lead you to prayer. Talk to God and ask him to come and show you his grace and your daily need of grace as you see areas where you need to grow. And second, let it lead you to seek out one or two people who love you and will walk with you as you seek to get a better idea of what can take hold of your heart and life more than your Savior. If you move in these two directions, the Spirit of God will certainly draw near and give you gracious self-awareness and enabling power to turn from the things that keep you from depending upon him.

Questions for Reflection

1. How did the beginning of this chapter encourage you as you started to read? How do you see God's Spirit at work in your life? If you can't, ask some trusted friends to help you see.

2. How did the challenge to engage in self-examination impact you? Did it make you more anxious, or were you hopeful? Why or why not?

3. As you began to engage in self-examination, what common themes do you notice in your life? What things tend to be "underneath" your worries? To what degree? For how long has this been the case?

4. How might "living in light of the kingdom of God" help you as you face your worries?

5. Write down two things that you tend to worry about and think through (or talk with a Christian friend about) how looking at the root cause of your worries is helpful, and how it is challenging.

8. Real Truths that Counter your Worry

Life is full of unexpected twists and turns. You really don't ever know what will happen next. And you do always know that you can't produce the outcomes that you want for yourself and your loved ones. And often, what happens is not what we would choose and the outcomes are not what we hoped for. And all this produces worry.

Since the Bible is a book about reality and dealing with reality, it acknowledges this. It is not a fairytale. The long narratives of Scripture and the emotive poetry of the prophets and psalms are saturated with heartache and painful loss. The Bible was written to and for people living in unpredictable times. It does not condone worry but it does understand why we worry. Life is hard no matter where you live. A friend of mine, who is an Old Testament scholar, said that over half of the Psalms could be categorized as psalms of lament. His conclusion from that simple observation is that much of life is lamentable. My friend, and the psalms, are correct.

No book on worry is worth its salt if it doesn't factor in the reality of suffering. But if there ever was a book that dealt honestly with suffering, it is the Bible. I have experienced suffering, and listened to countless stories from people I have counseled about suffering—stories that would bring you to tears. What separates those who grow in the midst of their suffering and those who don't is determined by what they thought about the presence of hardship and evil in the world and in their own lives.

That is what we will think about in this chapter. How does the God of the Bible speak to and address our common condition? How will we live in this world as it is, without resorting to worrying?

Short and Unpredictable

One of the obvious aspects of not being God is that we are not all-knowing (omniscient). As human beings, we are finite. However, as sinners, we can often grasp for infinite knowledge and aspire to be God. In the New Testament letter that bears his name, James writes as a pastor to people who are suffering a great deal. The entire letter is his loving counsel about how to live amid the uncertainty and not give in to the wide range of temptations to sin. Here is his counsel:

> Now listen, you who say, "Today or tomorrow we will go to this or that city, spend a year there, carry on business and make money." Why, you do not even know what will happen tomorrow. What is your life? You are a mist that appears for a little while and then vanishes. Instead, you ought to say, "If it is the Lord's will, we will live and do this or that." As it is, you boast in your arrogant schemes. All such boasting is evil. If anyone, then, knows the good they ought to do and doesn't do it, it is sin for them.   (James 4 v 13-17)

Some of James' original readers were falling into the temptation of acting as if the solution to their fear of the unknown future was an arrogant bravado of certainty. James is talking about an attitude of life, not simply about business and money. In an effort to overcome their anxieties, people pretend to be—even convince themselves they are—in complete control. This is not an uncommon response to the unpredictability of life. You may have tried to combat your anxiety through locating a portion of life in your universe (a tiny portion at that) where you feel you are in control (this is often at the root of many Obsessive Compulsive Disorders, OCD).

How does James seek to correct this kind of mindset? First, he reminds them that life is very unpredictable. "You do not even know what will happen tomorrow" (v 14). Second, he reminds them that life is very short. "What is your life? You are a mist that appears for a little while and then vanishes" (v 14). Wow! James does not hold anything back. He is a very direct pastor! He pushes things way beyond not knowing about what tomorrow will bring. He tells them they don't even know when they will die. Talk about comforting words!

And yet, they really are comforting! In essence, he is saying that a wise person lives with a healthy awareness that there are no guarantees between now and tomorrow. In fact, you don't have any guarantees that you will breathe another breath! You see, while life's unpredictability may lead someone to uncontrollable anxiety, James is using it to bring his flock to a place of sanity and calm. If you struggle with anxiety, at some level it is because you are recognizing something that is true about life in a broken world. Your problem, though, is that a helpful understanding that life is short and unpredictable has become an "over-concern." You have recognized that you are not someone who knows everything or controls everything; but you have not remembered that there is Someone who does! That is where James goes next.

A Vital "If"

James is able to speak so candidly because he doesn't stop with his emphasis on life's fragility. He replaces an arrogant attitude that erases God from the equation with an attitude of humility where God is at the center of the way you live your life: "Instead, you ought to say, 'If it is the Lord's will, we will live and do this or that'" (v 15). It is important to stress that James is not advising you to utter pious phrases at the start of your sentences; he is actually helping you to develop a way of thinking, believing and relating to God as you go about your daily life. James is encouraging you to live life *coram deo*: "before the face of God."

It is so tempting to go about your life functioning as if God is not real—under the pressure of needing to be in control, or experiencing the panic that you are not. This is true of people who don't believe in God—but it is also the functional approach of many who do. We can get up in the morning, eat, go about our business, interact with people, write and return emails, text others, or spend time alone— and never intentionally interact with God at all. This may give us a sense of confidence or of anxiety; either way, it is actually quite arrogant and spiritually dangerous. James calls it "boasting," because it is self-reliant (whether we conclude that we can rely on ourselves or that we can't). He actually calls it "evil."

What James is encouraging is a life lived with a clear sense of its fragility due to the reality and devastating impact of sin in the world. Along with that, he encourages dependence upon God: talking to him and acknowledging him throughout every moment of your existence. This is godly concern—wise action and dependent prayer. As you live your life, remember that while you are not all-knowing and all-powerful, you do belong to Someone who is—and that he wants you to rest in that fact and talk to him in the midst of your circumstances.

Suffering Will Come

It is not simply uncertainty that worries us; it is the possibility of suffering, too. And again, the Bible is both starkly realistic and greatly encouraging. While James says: *Yes, life is fragile,* Peter and Paul tell us: *Yes, you are going to suffer.*

Listen to Peter as he writes to Christians who are facing suffering and persecution at the hands of the Roman political authorities:

> Dear friends, do not be surprised at the fiery ordeal
> that has come on you to test you, as though something
> strange were happening to you.   (1 Peter 4 v 12)

Don't be surprised? Are you kidding?! Does Peter actually think this is going to help his readers? He absolutely does! For Peter, preparation is the key not just to survival but to growth and godly perseverance. Previously, Peter had been a very unstable disciple. He was constantly putting his foot in his mouth, and Jesus was regularly challenging him. But as an older, more mature believer, Peter has learned from his Master, Jesus, who regularly reminded his disciples that they were not above their Master. If he suffered, so would they, and so will you and I (John 13 v 15).

In light of that, how many of your trials are made more complicated by the way you respond to them? We have a way of making our troubles more troubling by how we respond. Often, it is because we are shocked when we suffer. Peter is preparing you for real life. Don't be surprised! This is what it means to be a human in a fallen world, and a Christian in a world that doesn't recognize Christ as King.

The Gift of Suffering

Paul takes this a step further. Listen to what he says in Philippians 1 v 29:

> For it has been granted to you on behalf of Christ not
> only to believe in him, but also to suffer for him.

The word that Paul uses when he says that it has been "granted" is a derivation of the Greek word *charis*. English Bibles translate it in most places as "grace" or "gift". Paul is saying that believing in Jesus and suffering for Jesus are two gifts that you receive when you are united to Christ. If you are like me, I am fine with the first gift but would rather return the second one! Christianity is a strange faith... or is it? Look at how other philosophies and religions deal with suffering. Most try to deny its existence or encourage a stoic acceptance of it. Not the Christian faith. It acknowledges the evil nature of suffering and at the same time redeems it for the good of the Christian sufferer. God promises to use it in your life and in the lives of others. Paul actually writes about his own sufferings in this way in 2 Corinthians 1 v 3-7:

> Praise be to the God and Father of our Lord Jesus
> Christ, the Father of compassion and the God of all
> comfort, who comforts us in all our troubles, so that
> we can comfort those in any trouble with the comfort
> we ourselves receive from God. For just as we share
> abundantly in the sufferings of Christ, so also our
> comfort abounds through Christ. If we are distressed, it
> is for your comfort and salvation; if we are comforted,
> it is for your comfort, which produces in you patient
> endurance of the same sufferings we suffer. And our
> hope for you is firm, because we know that just as you
> share in our sufferings, so also you share in our comfort.

Paul is saying that he has known God's comfort in his troubles. But not only that—because he has been troubled and known comfort, he is now in a position to comfort others. God has done in Paul what he promised through Paul in Romans 8 v 28: he has worked for his good, making him more like Christ, in "all things."

C. S. Lewis captured one aspect of this truth well in *Mere Christianity*. In an attempt to help a young Christian come to terms with ongoing suffering as part of the Christian life, he says this:

"That is why we must not be surprised if we are in for a rough time. When a man turns to Christ and seems to be getting on pretty well (in the sense that some of his bad habits are now corrected), he often feels that it would now be natural if things went fairly smoothly. When troubles come along—illnesses, money troubles, new kinds of temptations—he is disappointed. These things, he feels, might have been necessary to rouse him and make him repent in his bad old days; but why now? Because God is forcing him on, or up, to a higher level: putting him into situations where he will have to be very much braver, or more patient, or more loving, than he ever dreamed of being before. It seems to us all unnecessary: but that is because we have not yet had the slightest notion of the tremendous thing he means to make of us ... Imagine yourself as a living house. God comes in to rebuild that house. At first, perhaps, you can understand what he is doing. He is getting the drains right and stopping the leaks in the roof and so on: you knew that those jobs needed doing and so you are not surprised. But presently he starts knocking the house about in a way that hurts abominably and does not seem to make sense. What on earth is he

> up to? The explanation is that he is building quite a
> different house from the one you thought of—throwing out
> a new wing here, putting on an extra floor there, running
> up towers, making courtyards. You thought you were going
> to be made into a decent little cottage: but he is building a
> palace. He intends to come and live in it himself."

Paul is not ignoring or belittling his suffering, or yours. But think how many of our worries are caused by the possibility of future suffering, or the experience of present suffering. And then think how differently we would feel if we could say: *Yes, suffering will come. No, suffering will not last forever, because in eternity I will be in glory. And this suffering is all being used for my good, to make me more like Jesus, and to make me more able to be of use to those around me.* Think how differently we would think if when a loved one suffered we did not worry, but resolved to show godly concern; so that we wouldn't lie awake filled with anxiety, but instead in dependent prayer, that God would bring our loved one to repentance, or grow them in grace.

Suffering will happen, and it is meant to drive you to God, not to worry. You can trust him with your past, future and present and be useful to others in the midst of it all.

The Worst of Times, the Best of Times

Life is hard. That goes without saying. The Bible writers want you to factor that into the way you think about your own life in such a way that you are prepared in advance, so that you are not caught by surprise when difficulty happens. They also want you to live with the knowledge that God is not a deity who goes AWOL, nor a capricious being who is playing tricks on you. He is sovereignly orchestrating what you are going through and is committed to using it for your good.

Is that really true? How can you truly believe this when anxieties are pressing on you? When in doubt, look to the worst event in human history, and ask if God was out of control or not committed to you. Look at the perfect Son of God being judicially murdered. The worst event in human history was woven in such a way that your salvation, healing and final redemption were purchased. God was and is for you. God is with you. He loves you. Jesus, God in the flesh, is sufficient evidence of that. At the very moment when Jesus was hanging on the cross, it seemed that God had lost control. It appeared to be the worst of times. Instead, he was in supreme control and he was ordering these terrible events for our good. In truth, it was the best of times.

And Jesus, God in the flesh, shows us how we live that out. The night before he died, knowing some of the suffering the next day would bring, Jesus was under the severest pressure. What did he do? He prayed, and he trusted his Father's sovereign plan: "Father, if you are willing, take this cup from me; yet not my will, but yours be done" (Luke 22 v 42)— *Father, what will happen tomorrow would not be my choice, but it is yours, and I trust you.*

And in the moments before he died, knowing death was near, Jesus was experiencing the most agonizing pain, spiritually as well as physically. What did he do? He prayed, and he trusted his Father's care: "Father, into your hands I commit my spirit" (Luke 23 v 46)—*Father, I need not be anxious even as I die, for I am in your good, strong, loving hands.*

This is how we can live, and how we are to live as God's children. It is for you to accept this and weave it into the way you wake up every morning and go about your day. May God strengthen you and encourage you as you fight the battle of anxiety, worry and fear.

Questions for Reflection

1. While knowing that suffering is a part of life, how does the Bible put that in a framework that you find helpful?

2. James is a loving pastor who is writing to his congregation. They are going through a lot of suffering. How can reading the book of James with this in mind help you understand and apply its truths to your life?

3. When you read the quote from C. S. Lewis, what was your reaction?

4. Think of a time of suffering you have recently gone through, or are going through right now? In what sense could it be a "gift"? How would viewing it this way have changed, or change, the way you felt/feel?

5. What one point stood out in this chapter? Take a moment and talk to your God about it. Ask him to help you trust him more.

9. How to Cast All your Anxiety on Him

Knowing, understanding and even remembering everything in all of the chapters you've read will not help you much, if at all.

Because what matters, of course, is that we actually *change*.

And yet change in the Christian life is so often elusive. You know you need to change. You want to change. You even know what needs to change, and how. If you've got this far in this book, I guess you are wanting to change so that you worry less, and rejoice more.

But... *how?*

The More you Know?

We tend to think that if we just know the right things, change will happen. It's the approach taken by the public service commercials on American TV. The commercial briefly describes the social problem (teenage pregnancy, obesity, heart disease, etc.) and then provides some helpful advice to address the problem. The commercial always ends with this statement: "The more you know." In other words, right thinking will lead to right behavior.

Many professing Christians approach the Christian life in the same way. If you struggle with worry, anxiety, fear, anger or addictions (you pick your problem), the best way to change is through awareness and information. The more you know...

And knowledge is important. If this weren't true, then writing and reading this book would be useless! Change won't come if we don't think rightly.

But equally, thinking rightly doesn't automatically produce change. I know how I ought to treat my wife; but sometimes, I don't treat her in the way I know I should. I know what the speed limit on the freeway is; that knowledge alone does not mean I will change my driving habits.

So, there must be another dynamic in addition to right thinking. What exactly is that additional dynamic? What will take the information that you have gathered and utilize it in such ways that change begins to happen and the anxiety that you struggle with begins to lose its grip over your life?

If you don't answer that question, you will be left with a view of change that is simply cognitive/behavioral; that is, right thinking leads to right living. That is a very popular approach in both secular and Christian circles. And Paul seems to agree!

> Do not conform to the pattern of this world, but be transformed by the renewing of your mind. Then you will be able to test and approve what God's will is—his good, pleasing and perfect will.   (Romans 12 v 2)

So renewing your mind leads to transformation, right? Not quite—because when Paul talks about the mind, he's talking not just about our intellectual capacity, but our inner person. He is describing the part of someone that makes them tick; the central core of who a person is and what they live for. This is what we discussed in the previous chapter. He is talking about the seat of affections. For Paul, if you are not changed at the core of who you are, change in your behavior will not follow. Real change begins at the level of what we honor, treasure, adore or functionally worship on a daily basis. This is how commentator William Hendricksen states it in his explanation of this phrase:

> "Paul does not say, 'Substitute one outward fashion for another.' That would be no solution, for the trouble with those who allow themselves to be fashioned after the pattern of this present (evil) age is deep-seated. What is needed is 'transformation,' inner change, the renewing of the mind, that is, not only of the organ of thinking and reasoning but of the inner disposition; better still, of the heart, the inner being."

John Calvin, in his *Institutes of the Christian Religion*, says this about the process of change:

> "We have given the first place to the doctrine in which our religion is contained, since our salvation begins with it. But, it must enter our hearts and pass along to our daily living, and so transform us into itself that it may not be unfruitful for us ... [The gospel's] efficacy ought to penetrate the inmost affections of the heart, take its seat in the soul and affect the whole man a hundred times more deeply than the cold exhortations of the philosophers!"

In other words, change must happen at a deeper level than just thinking and behaving.

The Relationship Issue

What does this look like practically? It is more than talking to yourself and trying to convince yourself to change. It involves more than telling yourself to not worry because it is wrong. It is more than thinking positive thoughts (even biblical ones). It is even more than reminding yourself of who you are in Christ! It involves talking to and relating to Christ in the midst of your anxieties, worries and fears. Since God is personal, change that he accomplishes in you will be the result of you relating to him personally as you struggle.

1 Peter 5 v 7 captures this truth in the simplest of ways: "Cast all your anxiety on him because he cares for you." It is simple, but profound. Here is what Peter says to those of us who worry and live anxious lives. We will take the next several pages to look at some key aspects of this crucial passage:

> Humble yourselves, therefore, under God's mighty hand, that he may lift you up in due time. Cast all your anxiety on him because he cares for you.
>
> Be alert and of sober mind. Your enemy the devil prowls around like a roaring lion looking for someone to devour. Resist him, standing firm in the faith, because you know that the family of believers throughout the world is undergoing the same kind of sufferings.
>
> And the God of all grace, who called you to his eternal glory in Christ, after you have suffered a little while, will himself restore you and make you strong, firm and steadfast. To him be the power for ever and ever. Amen.
>
> (1 Peter 5 v 6-11)

Do you see what Peter is saying? He is encouraging you to relate to God in the very midst of your struggle with worry. *Talk to God,* he says: *Throw your worries and burdens on him. Know that he is more than a concept or a thought, he is a person. He cares for you!*

Here is the right way to approach change: right relating to God based upon right thinking about God will lead to right living before God. This does not mean it will be easy as you face your worries, nor does it mean that it will happen automatically or quickly. Rather, it will happen progressively over time. But it will happen. When you are struggling with anxiety, you must talk to and relate to God. There is no other way to experience lasting, abiding change, for this is the only way to change our hearts.

He Cares for You

Anxiety can flood into your life from many angles. We have talked about the past, present and future. Worry tempts us to think God does not care or he is not in control. This is not an innocent thought—it is a form of treason. Does that sound too strong? Consider this: if God did not spare his own Son for you, but gave him up for you, and you still doubt his goodness, love and mercy, this is a heart problem (Romans 8 v 32). If someone risked their life to save you from drowning and you were to ask them the next day: "Do you really care about me?" they would rightly feel insulted. God who gave his Son for you cares for you. He bore your sins. Will he not also carry your worries and burdens? Of course he will. So cast them on him instead of bearing them yourself. But what does this actually look like?

1. **Humble yourself:** If you think you can order your life and the universe better than God, you have a pride problem! Humble yourself: remind yourself of, and confess to God, who he is, who you are, and who you are not.
2. **Cast your anxieties on him:** This literally means "throw them on God once for all." This does not mean

that you can do it once and they will all dissipate. No, you have to do this daily. Stop. Sit down. Acknowledge what you are worrying about and begin to talk to God about it. Throw those cares upon him. Give them to him. Seek to leave them with him. Think about his wisdom, care and love for you in Christ, and give them to him. He cares for you.

The Spiritual Battle Behind Anxiety

In the same way that God is personal, to be acknowledged and worshiped, there is also a personal devil, to be resisted.

Whenever there is an area of vulnerability and weakness in the life of a Christian, the devil will certainly attempt to use this to his advantage. If you struggle with anxiety, it is a sign that you are not convinced that God really cares for you and will protect you. The evil one wants to exploit that inner vulnerability to such a degree that you feel isolated and alone. The devil is called "the accuser of our brothers and sisters" (Revelation 12 v 10). "Accuser" is legal language. Satan brings a case against you and says that you don't really find favor in God's eyes, because of who you are and what you have done. He is a guilt-producing prosecutor.

The only way to fight an unscrupulous lawyer is to find a better one! Thankfully, in Jesus, that is exactly what you have. Jesus is called our "advocate" (1 John 2 v 1); he is your lawyer. Jesus stands before our Father in heaven and makes a case for you. He successfully states that you are innocent before the Judge of heaven and earth because he has paid the price for your sins. You are not guilty. When you feel attacked by the evil one—when he tells you you're on your own, or unforgiven, or that life is out of control—tell him to take it up with your divine attorney, Jesus.

Firm in the Faith

Because it is so easy for you to forget the grace of God, especially in a season of worry, Peter reminds you to stand "firm in the faith" (1 Peter 5 v 9). The Christian life is a life that relies on grace—God's undeserved kindness—from beginning to end. This grace is freely given to us, but must be received daily by faith. You never wean yourself from God's grace. You don't start the Christian life by grace and then continue in it by your own performance. While you do exert energy as you grow in grace, that very energy is a work of God's grace in you (Philippians 2 v 12-13). I like how Peter says that you "stand" in faith. You don't lie down or sleep. You actively grow as a Christian as you stand in faith. The active Christian life is grounded in faith. Your activity is energized by God's work in you, and it will never add to or subtract from your firm footing before God because of who you are in Christ. You "stand" because you are confident in God's grace, which you have been freely given in Christ.

Part of the Family

In 1 Peter 5 v 9, Peter reminds us that we don't live alone: we are part of "the family of believers throughout the world." That means that we mustn't think we can grow very much (or at all) if we struggle alone; and it also means that we don't need to try to. We have brothers and sisters in Christ who are struggling in the same ways as we are. We can be open with each other. We can pray for and with each other. We can support and encourage and comfort and sometimes rebuke one another.

God calls us to change as part of his people. You cannot live and grow as a Christian on your own. You need others around you, encouraging you, praying for you, warning you and loving you. In order for this to happen, you need to have Christian friends who love you and know you well. You need to give them permission to challenge you at the same time as they pray for and encourage you. You need to ask them not to help you make excuses when you are worrying. If worry is an expression of not trusting God or not believing that he cares, that is a serious problem that cannot be ignored or overlooked. It's as we live in the family that we are encouraged and exhorted to grow more and more like our brother Jesus.

Putting it all Together: Meditation

The Bible is a book that is designed to forge a relationship between you and God, not simply to disseminate information. When I was a new Christian, someone described the Bible as a love letter to me from God. That is precisely correct. The Bible is not an encyclopedia or a cold history book. It is a letter that God has written that enables you to get to know him in the same way that you would get to know someone through conversation.

The word that best captures what this looks like in the Christian life is *meditation*. This word can be confusing, because of the way in which the term is often used. In Eastern religious traditions, meditation is a form of emptying your mind and uttering a "mantra" repeatedly as you seek to connect with the impersonal other. For the Christian, meditation is completely different. Christian meditation involves filling the mind with truth from the Bible and using that as a basis upon which to talk to our personal God. Truth is important; but it is a means to an end, and that end is relationship with Father, Son and Holy Spirit.

So, how do we meditate when we are tempted to worry? The Psalms are one ideal place where you find someone relating to God through mediation. I just scanned the first 100 psalms and found at least 22 that would be helpful for someone to meditate upon if they were struggling with worry (11; 13; 17; 18; 20; 22; 23; 25; 27; 31; 37; 43; 46; 55; 57; 64; 69; 71; 77; 86; 88; 91). Many of the psalms are a picture of someone relating to God in the midst of anxiety. Any part of the Bible can be used meditatively, but for the rest of the chapter, let's walk through Psalm 27 together and see how it can help us relate to God when we are, or could easily become, anxious.

Stanza One: Living in God's world

> The LORD is my light and my salvation—
>   whom shall I fear?
> The LORD is the stronghold of my life—
>   of whom shall I be afraid? (v 1)

The writer immediately re-orients you to remember that you live in God's world. You are not alone; God not only exists, but he loves you and knows you by name. Take a moment and put these truths into your own words as you talk to God. Go ahead! Do it now. If it feels awkward, that's okay. Talking to God does not come naturally to many of us. Ask God to help you talk to him.

Stanza Two: Name your Worries

> When the wicked advance against me
>   to devour me,
> it is my enemies and my foes
>   who will stumble and fall.
> Though an army besiege me,
>   my heart will not fear;

> though war break out against me,
>> even then I will be confident. (v 2-3)

Name the things that you are fearful of. Detail and name what you are worried about. Is it another person or a group of people? Is it your finances? What about your health? Whatever it is, name it and thank God that, in Christ, you are safe even if you should suffer any harm. Remember, being a Christian does not mean that you will avoid hardship and hurt. It does mean that God is present with you in the midst of your anxiety.

Stanza Three: God's Redeeming Grace

> One thing I ask from the LORD,
>> this only do I seek:
> that I may dwell in the house of the LORD
>> all the days of my life,
> to gaze on the beauty of the LORD
>> and to seek him in his temple.
> For in the day of trouble
>> he will keep me safe in his dwelling;
> he will hide me in the shelter of his sacred tent
>> and set me high upon a rock. (v 4-5)

The psalm begins by reminding you that you are living in God's world. The second section gives you the opportunity to voice your anxieties and name them. This next section focuses your attention on God's redeeming grace in the midst of your worry. When the writer talks about gazing upon the beauty of the LORD, it is a way of talking about God's wonderful mercy to forgive and redeem people who are weak and unworthy. The psalmist is reminded of God's blood sacrifice, which was re-enacted daily in the temple.

This, ultimately, points to God's saving mercies in Jesus (Hebrews 9). Take some time and let these words shape your conversation with God, expressing gratitude for his love for you in Christ. The life, death and resurrection of Christ is a bold reminder that God cares for you even though life is hard and you are anxious.

Stanza Four: God's Protection

Then my head will be exalted
    above the enemies who surround me;
at his sacred tent I will sacrifice with shouts of joy;
    I will sing and make music to the LORD. (v 6)

While we are not promised the absence of trial and suffering, we are promised that we will make it through to the other side and nothing can hinder that. Ultimately, nothing, not even evil-doers, will triumph over you. God will have the last word over your life and that word is grace. Take a moment to give thanks to God that he is protecting you from anything and everyone. Rejoice in conversation with God about this.

Stanza Five: Approach God Boldly

Hear my voice when I call, LORD;
    be merciful to me and answer me.
My heart says of you, "Seek his face!"
    Your face, LORD, I will seek.
Do not hide your face from me,
    do not turn your servant away in anger;
    you have been my helper.
Do not reject me or forsake me,
    God my Savior. (v 7-9)

As you can see, once the writer begins to meditate on God's mercy displayed in the temple (this is a foreshadowing of Jesus, the ultimate sacrifice), he cannot contain himself. Because of God's steadfast love, the singer of the psalm is having his priorities rearranged. While life in this world is hard and there are many things about which to be anxious, your sole place of orientation will be the reality of God's face. You can gaze upon him because he is real and he has made it possible for you to do so. Seeking the face of God is a bold statement in the Old Testament, particularly in light of how many times people are utterly undone before the face of God. Take a moment and talk to God, and give thanks that you can approach him with this kind of confidence and move towards him without fear of rejection or judgment.

Stanza Six: Back to Real Life with Confidence

Though my father and mother forsake me,
　　the LORD will receive me.
Teach me your way, LORD;
　　lead me in a straight path
　　because of my oppressors.
Do not turn me over to the desire of my foes,
　　for false witnesses rise up against me,
　　spouting malicious accusations. (v 10-12)

Now the psalm returns to life in the real world and begins to contemplate a different set of possible hardships that would all be anxiety-producing. The writer even refers to injustices that may be committed against him. His confidence in God's steadfast love for him has been etched into his mind, and the roots of that love have sunk deeper into his heart to such a degree that he can actually name more potential harmful things and do so with greater confidence. Take some time and root your heart in God's love for you. Thank God for this. Begin to name potential trials that may be a part of your life and face them down with confidence, because Christ has overcome sin, death and hell for you.

Stanza Seven: Ultimate Triumph

> I remain confident of this:
>> I will see the goodness of the LORD
>> in the land of the living.
> Wait for the LORD;
>> be strong and take heart
>> and wait for the LORD. (v 13-14)

The psalm ends with added confidence in God's ultimate victory over anything and everyone who would stand in his way. God will triumph and you can remain content and patient in the face of adversity. You can fight against any anxiety that may be creeping into your life right now. You can do this because you know the end of the story. Revelation 20 – 21 tells us that God will bring all things to their conclusion in such a way that justice will be maintained and mercy will be displayed to those who have bowed the knee to King Jesus.

Real Change, but not a Quick Fix

This example is meant to model true Christian meditation. It is not a cognitive exercise that promises a quick fix to your struggle with worry. This one example will be something that you will need to model for your entire life, each day. This is living life in relationship with Father, Son and Spirit. This is the rhythm of your Christian existence.

As much as we would love instantaneous results and deliverance from our struggles, God loves a dependent, child-like faith that walks hand in hand with him daily. My experience of change in my own life, and the change I have watched happening in others', is usually slow, with lots of ups and downs. Sometimes it is even hard to know if I am making any progress because I find myself failing over and over again. Maybe you find the same thing. Don't be discouraged, though. If you belong to God, the trajectory will be upward. While you will never "arrive" until Christ returns or you go to be with him, remember that he is walking with you and change is happening even if you can't always see it. You can change. You will change. And you will do it as you walk hand in hand with your Father, not just knowing his promises but trusting them, treasuring them, and living by them. If this is the pattern of your life with God, you will experience change over time.

Questions for Reflection

1. Have you ever thought about the difference between change that is based upon right knowledge and change that is based upon a relationship with God?

2. What things are you tempted to keep in your grasp rather than casting them on God?

3. When was the last time you actually prayed against the work of the evil one over your life, and rested more confidently in Jesus' defense of you as your attorney? Do you need to do so now?

4. What will it look like for you to be active in your fight against worry? Gather a few close friends and ask them to pray with and for you. Ask them to check in on you to see how you are doing.

5. Pick one of the psalms mentioned in this chapter and use it as a basis for relating to God in the way that Psalm 27 is used—or, if you would rather, use Psalm 27 and the content of this chapter.

10. What Would Jesus Say?

The Bible is about real, normal people, and how God meets those normal people in real ways. In this chapter, we'll listen in together on how the Lord counsels a fearful man who had a great deal, humanly speaking, to be anxious about.

Weak, Fearful, Trembling

In Acts 18, we find Paul near the end of his second of three missionary journeys. He leaves Athens, Greece, and is on his way to the city of Corinth. As far as we know, his time in Athens was not terribly successful, since we have no account of a church being started there. Here is how Paul describes how he felt as he travelled to Corinth:

> I came to you in weakness with great fear and trembling.
>
> (1 Corinthians 2 v 3)

Corinth was a very modern city that served as a hub for commerce from all over that part of the world. It was a very immoral city, too. It was not going to be easy to see a church movement take hold in Corinth and the failures in Athens were no doubt on Paul's mind. Paul was struggling with anxiety.

It's understandable, when you consider all that Paul has been through by this point. Consider if you might be a bit worried if you had experienced the following:

- Being stoned (Acts 14 v 19-20)
- Being flogged (16 v 22-23)
- Spending time in prison (16 v 16-40)
- Betrayal by friends with whom you have shared the joys and challenges of ministry (15 v 36-41)
- Harassment and persecution by those who used to respect and like you (18 v 12-13)

On top of all of this, as Paul arrives in Corinth, he is running low on money so he must work another job during the week (18 v 3), and he arrives alone. Paul was living in ripe conditions for worry to well up in his life.

What About You?

Maybe you are facing a very difficult financial problem and your resources are not able to cover what is needed. Perhaps someone at work has slandered you and your job is in question. Or maybe you lost a loved one and you are wondering how you will move forward in your life without them. Whatever the circumstances, you know what Paul is experiencing because one way or another you have been there, too. While your experience may or may not be similar by degrees, it is anxiety-producing just the same. See, Paul is no super-saint with whom you cannot identify. No, he is just like you. He was a man who experienced deep joys and success in life but also great weakness, defeat and failure. He, like you, struggled with deep worry.

I was speaking to a friend recently who was going through a long separation and divorce from his wife. Her behavior had become quite erratic and she had accused him of all sorts of things. In the middle of all of this were several children who were suffering as well. He did not know what to do. Sadly, he found himself more and more isolated, because people did not want to be associated with him and his situation. Eventually, the divorce was finalized, but the saga is far from over. He still has to think about how he can care for his children. He has added financial responsibilities and work is hard to find in his field of employment. How can he move forward in the midst of what has happened as well as what may well lie ahead? What will enable him to move ahead and face his fears?

My friend needs the same thing that helped Paul. You and I do, too. How did the Lord help Paul?

Do not be Afraid

Here is what the Jesus said to Paul in a vision:

> "Do not be afraid; keep on speaking, do not be silent. For I am with you, and no one is going to attack and harm you, because I have many people in this city." So Paul stayed in Corinth for a year and a half, teaching them the word of God. (Acts 18 v 9-11)

"Do not be afraid." These are words that you will find throughout the pages of the Bible. And while this may have been a face-to-face encounter with the risen Jesus that you and I probably will not enjoy this side of heaven, the command and comfort are the same. Jesus is simply repeating to Paul the same consistent message that he gives to his people throughout history. He quite simply and yet profoundly says: *Do not worry.*

His command encourages Paul to keep doing what he has been doing. *Don't waver one bit,* Jesus is saying: *Don't be afraid; keep on speaking, do not be silent.* Anxiety often leads to disobedience, because it tells us God does not care or is not in control, so he cannot be trusted with our lives and futures. Fight or flight kicks in. In Paul's case, the temptation he faces is to shut down and give up. After all the lack of success, it would be tempting to throw in the towel and go on vacation. *No*, says Jesus to Paul: *Keep on preaching the gospel. Press into your fears and move forward.* This feels as if Jesus is just telling Paul to "grin and bear it," maintain a "stiff upper lip," or "keep calm and carry on." But Jesus is commanding Paul to do something more than that. He is calling Paul to live by faith. What does that mean? Faith involves doing the very opposite of what comes naturally. And sometimes it feels wooden and insincere, but it is not. Don't be fooled by your mere emotions. While it is often good to have your emotions right in step with your behavior, it is not always the case.

In order to fully appreciate Jesus' counsel, you must consider who is speaking to Paul and how he is speaking. This changes everything. When God speaks commands to a believer, the context is that of a parent speaking to a child. Let me explain. When my children were young, occasionally one would have a bad dream and come running into our room. Barbara and I would awaken to a frightened child, and we would say: "Don't be afraid." If you are a parent, you know the intention and the tone that would be conveyed in those words. They would be gentle and reassuring, not harsh and shaming. If you are a child of the Father, his loving commands are words of encouragement and grace, not words of shame. He loves you and is concerned for your well-being. He is actually saying: *My dear child, I know you are frightened and I hear your cries and sense how afraid you are, but don't be afraid, my child. You belong to me, I am here with you, and I will take care of you.* These are not the commands of a dictator but of a loving Father.

Let's keep following Jesus' counsel. After Jesus gives Paul this command, he then gives him three reasons that will enable him joyfully to obey it. There are many reasons for Paul to be anxious; and there are three great reasons why he does not need to be, and should not be. This is how the Bible always works. A command is always grounded in reasons.

Reason One: "For I am with you"

If you are a Christian, you are in a relationship with the living God based solely upon what Jesus has done for you in his life, death and resurrection. Your sins have been forgiven. You have been given the perfect record of Jesus. You have been embraced by the One who had every right to reject you. He is your Father and you are his child. When he speaks to you through the Bible, he is speaking words of hope, encouragement and grace. Consider the following words and notice how a relationship with Jesus is connected to obeying his commands:

> As the Father has loved me, so have I loved you. Now remain in my love. If you keep my commands, you will remain in my love, just as I have kept my Father's commands and remain in his love. I have told you this so that my joy may be in you and that your joy may be complete.   (John 15 v 9-11)

You have to get the order right. Obedience to the Father starts with your relationship with him, not the other way around. You don't obey so that you can earn his love. But the more you obey, the deeper your experience of his love becomes.

Reason Two: "And No One is Going to Attack and Harm you"

Consider these encouraging words. Of course, not all of us can know that no one will harm us, in this specific way. But we can know what Jesus says in Matthew 10 v 28:

> Do not be afraid of those who kill the body but cannot
> kill the soul. Rather, be afraid of the One who can
> destroy both soul and body in hell.

While we are not guaranteed complete safety from attacks and harm in this life, we do belong to the One who has the power to raise our bodies and souls to new life at the resurrection of those who die in Christ.

Reason Three: I have Many People in this City

This third reason is actually a call to "seek first [God's] kingdom" (Matthew 6 v 33). Jesus is encouraging Paul to be busy about spreading the good news of the kingdom of God. He is saying: *Let that be your primary drive. Let nothing deter you from that single focus. Set your heart on the work I am doing and I will take care of you.* Jesus encourages Paul to view Corinth through a different lens. He is calling Paul, and you, to look at his situation and circumstances through a different lens. In essence, Jesus is saying: *Paul, don't look at Corinth as a city full of enemies. Look at Corinth through eyes that see this city full of future friends and brothers and sisters in Christ! Look at Corinth through my eyes, Paul.*

What are you facing right now that feels insurmountable? Is there something that God is calling you to do that scares you to death? Does someone need you to move in their direction but you can't seem to find the resolve to go there, because you fear it won't turn out right? Many times, we avoid opportunities because of fear. We are looking at the situation through a lens that is distorted. You need Jesus to counsel you as he did Paul.

The Worry-spiral and its Antidote

There is a worry-spiral that we can go down, that we need Jesus to help us out of. It's what we find him doing here for Paul:

- *Phase 1:* Worry and Fear—God gets smaller and other people and your situation begin to overwhelm you. *Do not be afraid!*
- *Phase 2:* Paralysis—You start shutting down and getting silent. You feel helpless and things feel out of control. *Keep on speaking; do not be silent!*
- *Phase 3:* Isolation—You start feeling as if you are all alone. You feel abandoned. God is remote and people have deserted you. *For I am with you!*
- *Phase 4:* Paranoia—Other people are scary. They are out to get you. They are not safe. *No one is going to attack and harm you!*
- *Phase 5:* Hopelessness—Nothing you do matters. Why bother? Why not just give up? *I have many people in this city!*

Jesus spoke to Paul to lift him out of this. And it worked— what did Paul do? He stayed in Corinth for a year and a half, preaching and teaching the word of God. The gospel took root in Corinth. People who became Christians were radically changed from their former way of life. Their lives were totally distinctive and quite impressive to outsiders. Imagine if Paul had allowed his worries to get the best of him!

Let Jesus Counsel You

Remember, the apostle Paul was a human being just like you are. He did not have any unique powers that you don't have. He lived in a very dangerous part of the world, at a time when safety was far less than it is in many of the places in the world today. His future was always uncertain, except for the certainty of suffering. He was weak, flawed and finite. And Jesus met him in his time of anxiety with some very simple but profound words of encouragement. Through this passage, he is speaking the same words to you. Through his promises, he is speaking to you as the one who went to the cross for you and who reigns in heaven for you, and he is saying lovingly, gently, but firmly:

"Do not worry."

Questions for Reflection

1. How is it both encouraging and challenging to be reminded that the apostle Paul was just an ordinary human being like you?

2. What do you think when you see the things Paul went through? Do you tend to have more compassion when you see that he struggled with fear? How should this impact the way you treat others or think about yourself when worry is pronounced?

3. Does anything surprise you about what Jesus says to Paul in the middle of his anxiety?

4. Take one area of anxiety, or potential anxiety, in your life. How do Jesus' command and promise guide you toward peace in that area?

5. Is your worry or fear threatening to hold you back from serving others? What will you do about this?

11. Conclusion

I hope this book has given you greater clarity about what your worry is and how you can begin to grow in grace, replacing your anxieties with peace. I hope you have seen that the Bible is rich in its description and understanding of worry—that even though you may not find the words "worry" or "anxiety" on every page of Scripture, the struggle is prevalent throughout its pages. And I hope that you have grasped more clearly that it is your relationship with Christ that is central to any true, lasting change.

We have considered Jesus' words in Matthew 6 several times, but I want to finish with Luke's account of those same words, and a single sentence that Luke alone records:

> Do not be afraid, little flock, for your Father has been pleased to give you the kingdom. (12 v 32)

Read that once again:

> Do not be afraid, little flock, for your Father has been pleased to give you the kingdom.

Do you see how Jesus speaks to you? As we finish, I want to leave you with three things from this line: the Lord's command for you, his reassurance of you, and his promise to you.

Do not be Afraid

Just as he did to Paul specifically in Corinth, Jesus commands his disciples in general—all of them—not to worry. Worry is a sign that you believe that God is not good or that he is not in charge, and that he therefore cannot be trusted to care for you.

So worrying is a very serious thing—it is a state of mind and soul that resists the truth about who God truly is. Don't minimize or excuse your worry as if it were okay, or inevitable. Jesus says it is sinful and that you ought not to do it. He does not mince words. Worry is the attempt to live in two kingdoms simultaneously and serve two masters at the same time. It can't be done. Your loyalty can only be to one kingdom at a time. Jesus loves you and he is clearly, uncompromisingly telling you that worry is wrong and that it is dangerous.

Little Flock

At the same time that Jesus speaks tough words and challenges you, he does so with a tone that is tender in its toughness, and compassionate in its candor. Don't let this little phrase that Jesus utters evade you. Don't miss those two powerful words: "little flock." While Jesus challenges you to not worry or fear, he speaks to you as one who belongs to him, whom he is shepherding and for whom he laid down his life. You are unimaginably dear to him and loved by him. You are one of his sheep. Be reassured—he cares for you and loves you even as you struggle with worry, even as you forget him and his care, and give in to your tendency to worry. You may be prone to wander, but you will always be part of his flock.

Your Father is Pleased to Give you the Kingdom

What would you do if you knew that you were going to inherit several billion dollars at some point in your life? How would that impact the way you lived? How would that change the way you thought about finances? It would be a game-changer! Not only would you not worry over paying the bills, you would be much more likely to be generous.

That is the point Jesus is making here. His command and his reassurance is followed by a promise to those who hear the command. Jesus says that your eternal "bank account" is secure. You have everything you need, and then some. You don't have to worry about this life, or the next. He will take care of you now and into the future. The kingdom is yours. You will enjoy the rich goods of life in God's presence. Your future life is one that cannot be described because it is indescribable.

C. S. Lewis puts it this way in the last of his *Chronicles of Narnia* books, *The Last Battle*, as the main characters stand before the Christ figure, Aslan, beyond their own deaths:

> "And as [Aslan] spoke he no longer looked to them like a lion; but the things that began to happen after that were so great and beautiful that I cannot write them. And for us this is the end of all the stories, and we can most truly say that they all lived happily ever after. But for them it was only the beginning of the real story. All their life in this world and all their adventures in Narnia had only been the cover and the title page: now at last they were beginning Chapter One of the Great Story, which no one on earth has read: which goes on forever: in which every chapter is better than the one before."

Your Father in heaven is able to, willing to, and pleased to give you things that are inexpressible and that defy the imagination. He has given you his kingdom. It is in you now by his Spirit, and you will live in it one day with him. So... do not worry.

Question for Reflection

As a result of reading this book, what has changed, or needs to change, in your:

- view of Jesus?
- perspective on your worries?
- attempts to change?
- prayers?
- counsel to others when they tell you they are worried about something?

Thank you...

Writing a book is hard work on the part of many, not just the author. In a spirit of humility and gratitude I would like thank the following people:

... my family: Barbara, Nate and Hannah, Tim, Kathryn and Benjamin. You are the family every father and husband should have. Thankfully, I do. You practice patience as I slowly grow in grace.

... our parents: Clyde and JoAnn Lane, and Bill and Sue Casey. A parent's work is never done. You four have been a source of strength.

... fellow friends and ministers in the gospel: Craig Higgins, Drew Derreth, Scot Sherman and Stuart Stogner. Our annual gatherings have been a source of encouragement and accountability over two decades of ministry. We have walked with one another through seasons of blessing and trial.

... Carl Laferton, my editor at The Good Book Company. It was a pleasure to work with you. Our spirited, candid and cordial back-and-forth over this manuscript made it far better than it would have ever been. Thanks for keeping me from "waggling at the tee" too much at the beginning of almost every chapter!

... Mike Harrell, Faye Marion and George Parry: fellow Georgians. Thank you for your wise counsel and guidance.

LIVEDIFFERENT

HONEST EVANGELISM

This is a book that is honest about the costs, and excited about the effects, of evangelism. And, as he draws on decades of experience, Rico shows how you—whoever you are and however you feel—can talk about Jesus with those who don't yet know him, but need to meet him.

Rico is one of the clearest and most faithful evangelists alive today. No one is in a better position to write this book. I can't wait to use Honest Evangelism.

PROF MICHAEL HORTON, AUTHOR OF *ORDINARY*

YOU CAN REALLY GROW

Most of us feel deep down that we ought to be growing as Christians. We are often told to grow as Christians. But... what is Christian growth? And how do we pursue it. In this refreshing, uplifting, and at times surprising book, you'll see why, and how, you really can really grow.

John Hindley

SERVING WITHOUT SINKING

John Hindley's debut, bestselling book shows what can happen as we do "Christian serving" that leads to discouraged or bitter hearts; and revolutionises our view of ourselves so that we can serve long, hard, sacrificially... and joyfully.

I keep finding myself in conversations with people who Serving Without Sinking addresses—people who serve, but are growing weary. It will be a great blessing to them—and to you.

TIM CHALLIES, PASTOR AND BLOGGER

Stephen Witmer

ETERNITY CHANGES EVERYTHING

Be amazed by what the Christian's future is, and be given confidence that it's *your* future; and then see how your future transforms your present, making you restlessly patient, dissatisfied yet content, and able to love more and live better.

www.thegoodbook.com/livedifferent

thegoodbook
COMPANY

Opening up the Bible

At The Good Book Company, we are dedicated to helping Christians and local churches grow. We believe that God's growth process always starts with hearing clearly what he has said to us through his timeless word—the Bible.

Ever since we opened our doors in 1991, we have been striving to produce resources that honor God in the way the Bible is used. We have grown to become an international provider of user-friendly resources to the Christian community, with believers of all backgrounds and denominations using our Bible studies, books, evangelistic resources, DVD-based courses and training events.

We want to equip ordinary Christians to live for Christ day by day, and churches to grow in their knowledge of God, their love for one another, and the effectiveness of their outreach.

Call us for a discussion of your needs or visit one of our local websites for more information on the resources and services we provide.

North America: www.thegoodbook.com
UK & Europe: www.thegoodbook.co.uk
Australia: www.thegoodbook.com.au
New Zealand: www.thegoodbook.co.nz

North America: 866 244 2165
UK & Europe: 0333 123 0880
Australia: (02) 6100 4211
New Zealand (+64) 3 343 1990

www.christianityexplored.org

Our partner site is a great place for those exploring the Christian faith, with a clear explanation of the good news, powerful testimonies and answers to difficult questions.

One life. What's it all about?